The Chi Kung Way

James MacRitchie is from Liverpool, England. A Chi Kung practitioner and teacher, he is co-director, with his wife Damaris Jarboux, of The Chi Kung School at The Body-Energy Center in Boulder, in the Rocky Mountains of Colorado. Jim also has a full-time practice of Classical Taoist Acupuncture and Chi Kung Healing at The Acupuncture Centre of Boulder. He is Founding President of The Chi Kung/Qigong Association of America, and a council member of The World Academic Society of Medical Qigong (Beijing).

Jim co-founded and directed The Evolving Institute – A Centre For Personal and Social Evolution (Boulder, 1982–88) and The Natural Dance Workshop (Europe, 1975–81). He has extensive experience in teaching, public speaking and leading workshops and events.

He is the author of *Chi Kung: Cultivating Personal Energy* (Element, 1993); *Exit-to-Enter* with Anna Halprin (San Francisco Dancers Workshop, 1973); *The State of Play: Theatre Games as Social Art* with Bill Harpe (Great Georges Community Arts Project, 1972). He contributed the Qigong chapter to *The Chinese Way to Health* by Dr Stephen Gascoigne MD. He publishes *The International Chi Kung/Qigong Directory*.

Jim did the illustrations for this book.

The Chi Kung Way

Alive with Energy

James MacRitchie

Thorsons

An Imprint of HarperCollins*Publishers*

Thorsons
An Imprint of HarperCollins*Publishers*
77–85 Fulham Palace Road
Hammersmith, London W6 8JB
1160 Battery Street
San Francisco, California 94111–1213

Published by Thorsons 1997

1 3 5 7 9 10 8 6 4 2

Line illustrations by the author

A catalogue record for this book
is available from the British Library

ISBN 0 7225 3025 0

Printed and bound in Great Britain by
Caledonian International Book Manufacturing Ltd, Glasgow

Contents

气 功

Foreword

Chi Kung makes people healthy, beautiful and gives long life.

In China, Chi Kung has developed for thousands of years – it is a crystallization of collective wisdom. People can use Chi Kung to help them stay healthy by adjusting their spirits, breath, organs, and other aspects of themselves. In recent years people have understood Chi Kung better, and found it easy to learn, so there are more and more teachers and it is spreading widely.

The new field of scientific Chi Kung researches the basic principles and effects of Chi Kung. Today it involves not only the study of subjective feelings, but also biology, electronics, electrochemistry, magnetism, enzymology, microwave and many other unitary and manifold sciences. Chi Kung is now a science of hi tech.

Foreword

The following conclusions have been proven from the perspective of immunology:

+ Chi Kung can help people keep healthy.
+ Chi Kung can help creatures and plants grow.
+ Chi Kung can prevent tumours from growing and cure them.
+ Chi Kung is material and its effects can be measured.
+ Chi Kung is energy information.

In the 21st century Chi Kung will be at the forefront of medicine. However, as well as its applications in science and medicine, Chi Kung emphasizes health, fitness, personal development and spiritual growth. It is of major value for the greater benefit of all the people of the world. This book is a good contribution to the development of Chi Kung.

Professor Feng, Lida, MD

Vice-President – The World Academic Society of Medical Qigong
Director – Immunology Research Centre
Beijing, China
February 1997

Preface

Alive with Energy

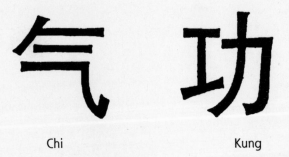

Chi   Kung

Chi means 'energy'.

Kung means 'working with', 'developing' or 'cultivating'.

Chi Kung means 'working with energy', 'developing energy' or 'cultivating energy'.

Preface

Chi Kung may be one of the most important things you ever learn. It has the power to transform your life, and, indeed, the whole of Western society. It could revolutionize what we think we are, how we think we work, and our relationship to each other and to the natural environment. It could change how we understand ourselves and live our lives. It has the potential to make us happy and to make us alive with energy.

How can this be so? How is this possible? Surely this is an exaggeration?

Well, for over 3,000 years Chi Kung has been one of the most closely guarded secrets of Oriental cultures and a cornerstone of those ancient civilizations. It is also known as Qi Gong, Chee Gung and Ji Kong. It is, in many ways, one of the missing pieces that we in the West have been looking for. It promises to provide the answers to some of the major questions that we have long been asking, and the solutions we have been seeking and now so urgently need. It could take our society the next quantum leap forward.

The practices of Chi Kung have applications across the whole spectrum of human experience – from sports to spirituality, from health care to sex, from ageing to heightened states of consciousness. It is relevant to education, medicine, recreation, psychology, mental health, business, art, science and personal development. It can unlock the hidden abilities that we all inherently have.

'Chi Kung' is like 'music' or 'dance' – it is an activity that people do. It can be considered the Chinese equivalent of yoga, which has a comparable range and scope. There are many kinds of Chi Kung – Five Animal Frolic Chi Kung, Healing Sounds Chi Kung, Eight Extra Meridian Chi Kung, Soaring Crane Chi Kung, and so on. There is a wide variety of forms, styles and traditions, with a broad range of applications and purposes. There are 'external' forms which involve postures, movement and physical exercise, and 'internal' forms which involve various kinds of meditation and energy practices. Some are ancient, originating before recorded history, some were created by contemporary teachers. There are widely known fitness sequences performed by large numbers of people in public in China and there are spiritual practices known as Inner Alchemy which are transmitted one-on-one from teacher to selected student.

The Chi Kung State

In Western terms Chi Kung is difficult to explain, because there is no comparison or parallel in our own culture. We have a very different understanding of what we are, how we work and how best to take care of ourselves. However, the body-energy system has been here all along because it is a primary biological system that we all have.

But it's not the words or intellectual understanding of Chi Kung that are important here – it's the experience. Chi Kung is something that a person has to *do* in order to know what the words mean, what the experience is and what it feels like. And the condition achieved as a result of the practice is called 'the Chi Kung State'.

We can be in many different 'states of being' – normal-every-day, stressed, excited, depressed, exhilarated, and so on. One of the problems we face is that our Western culture does not have comprehensive criteria or a reference point of our *best* state, not least because we do not include body-energy in the picture.

So what is the Chi Kung State? It is a heightened state of being. Characteristics of this state are feeling calm, clear, relaxed, aware, strong, centred, whole, integrated, balanced and fully alive – to name but a few.

This state simply feels better than any other. Athletes and dancers are in it often. It could be a new definition of the most desirable state to be in.

This Book

In 1993 I wrote a book entitled *Chi Kung: Cultivating Personal Energy* (Element Books). It was an introductory, comprehensive overview, written in a simple, straightforward, common language. The book was very favourably received and has become established as a basic textbook in the field.

For people familiar with the first book, this new book is the next step – a developmental progression. While the first book contained only six Chi Kung practices, this contains 65, covering the whole range of possible ways of doing Chi Kung from energy-massage to spiritual development. Where it covers, by necessity, similar basic theoretical material, this information has been revised and expanded.

However, this book is also a complete textbook in itself. It explains clearly and completely what Chi Kung is and how it works. It also includes a wide range of exercises and practices which anybody in average health can do, regardless of previous experience. For people who are new to Chi Kung it will provide a thorough introduction, while for people who are already familiar with this invaluable art it will present new information and fresh ways of thinking about and doing the practices.

In recent years there has been an enormous upsurge of interest and activity in what is called 'energy healing'. A bewildering assortment of different forms, styles and techniques has emerged – reiki, therapeutic touch, jin shin, healing touch, shiatsu, acupressure, do in, chakra balancing, spiritual healing... Chi Kung provides a practical, technical, down-to-earth basis for making sense of all of these – and the common link between them.

This book is about the practices and exercises of Chi Kung which can make it a part of our everyday life. By practising Chi Kung you can experience and develop your own energy and life, and, through this mysterious and wonderful ancient art, become Alive with Energy!

A Personal Odyssey

On a more personal note, this book is the result of a 25-year odyssey to discover the essence of body-energy – half of my lifetime. So far this journey has involved the formal study of classical Taoist acupuncture and 20 years of practice; training and dialogue with a wide variety of Chi Kung and other teachers; 15 years of teaching; and travels in Europe, the USA and China. Along the way it has resulted in establishing The Chi Kung School at The Body-Energy Center in Boulder, Colorado, producing public conferences in body-energy, writing *Chi Kung: Cultivating Personal Energy* and publishing *The International Chi Kung/Qigong Directory*. In 1993 I was appointed a council member of the World Academic Society of Medical Qigong (Beijing). In 1996 I was elected Founding President of the Chi Kung/Qigong Association of America – the first national association. The quest continues...

I most sincerely hope that this book not only informs you about Chi Kung but also inspires you to practise it and make it part of everyday life. Practising Chi Kung is one of the best things that anybody can possibly do for themselves. It is one of the most practical and effective processes ever developed by humankind for personal and social evolution. And it is all available to you, right now! It is already yours. All you have to do is learn it, make it your own, and *practise...*

James MacRitchie

The Chi Kung School at The Body-Energy Center,
Boulder, Colorado
26 February, 1997

This book is dedicated, with my love,
to my wonderful wife and Chi partner,
Damaris Jarboux

Acknowledgements

Any book of this nature is the result of contributions, help and inspiration of many people. Acknowledgement, thanks and credit are due to the following.

For proofreading and assistance at various stages of writing: Andrea Arduine, Teresa Banta, Laura Barnard, Sloan Bashinsky, Kim Bradshaw, Elisabeth Culley, Jeanie Daniel, Frank French, Susan Horanic, Judy Jacobsen, Margaret Johnson, Michael Kubitschek, Amy Newfeld, Andrew Nugent-Head, Randall Rothberg, Jerry Ryan, Pamela Severance, John Smaine, Randi R. G. Stroh, Carolyn Stollman, Dr Morton Walker, Vayu and Zhu Xilin. For providing invaluable support and encouragement along the way: Betsy Albright, Professor Ting Yu Fang, Bill Harpe, Debra and Craig Harris, Karen, Peggy and Josh at The Mailbox, Jefree Kaufman, Hong Liu, Robert B. McFarland MD, Richard Ruster PhD, Eddie and Debbie Shapiro, David Scott PhD, Jill Wilkins and Ms Hua Yuan. To my major Chi Kung and other teachers: Guo Guang Chen, Mantak Chia, Gareth Davis, Shou Yu Liang, Hoe V. Nyugen, Gunther Weil, Pao Chin Huang, Su Jian Wan, J. R. Worsley, my fellow practitioners, and the many students who, over the years, have helped develop the ideas and practices in this book. My special thanks and acknowledgement to my teaching associate Jesse Dammann, and to four-year-old Petra Hollingshead for being so *Alive with Energy*. To the people who helped with the production: my literary agent Susan Mears, Rick Fields for his consultations, and all the people at HarperCollins who assisted in bringing this into being in many ways – Sarah Sutton, Erica Smith, Michelle Pilley, Michelle Turney, Louise McNamara, Lizzie Hutchins, Christina Digby, Paul Redhead, Jo Ridgeway and everyone else who helped. Thanks folks. And, of course, to my family, for their unending support and love: my mother Joan Frederica Tilley, children Sonnet, Hagan and John, sister Susan, brother Malcolm and all my extended family.

Professor Wang, Jin Hai for his calligraphy of The Tao.

The practices in this book have been adapted and modified from various sources and teachings of particular individuals, and have been refined over 14 years of teaching.

The exercises and practices in this book are not a substitute for medical treatment. If you have a medical condition, see a medical doctor.

气 功

Introduction

Back to the Future

'Do you want to hear the good news or the bad news?' It's an age-old question. And every age has its answers.

As we approach the millennium there sometimes seems to be a superabundance of bad news and a remarkably small amount of good news. And not only is good news hard to find, but bad news may even disguise itself as good news.

For instance, those of us who live in the most developed of countries may fail to recognize that we are among the most deprived people on Earth. We buy our vegetables, we don't grow them. We buy our bread, we don't bake it. We buy our Christmas cards and birthday cards and clothes, we don't design and make them ourselves. We buy our music on cassette and disc. And we buy our cars, computers, TVs, food processors and washing machines – and usually don't know how to service or repair them. It seems that we are being programmed for consuming rather than creating, that we are increasingly be-coming 'viewers' rather than 'doers'. So it's not surprising if we come to believe that our health is also somebody else's business and outside our control.

But in the midst of all this emphasis on the wealthiest citizens of the world living out their lives as passive consumers, there is also good news. And this book is one such message. For James MacRitchie is someone who believes that our good health is, first and foremost, our own business and should be under our control. And he has written this book to explain not only why he believes this but also how we can all achieve it.

Now, if you are convinced that responsibility for healthcare is a matter for experts – who examine, test, diagnose and subse-quently treat generally passive patients – then you are in for a surprise. But if you are of the inclination that you should take control of your own mental, spiritual and physical well-being, then this book could be the stimulus for a great awakening.

Not that this compact, readable and down-to-earth work is filled with the latest medical and scientific discoveries. For, while the wisdom James MacRitchie presents in his book has been filtered through twentieth-century theory and practice, it also comes with a 2,000-year plus guarantee. Indeed, this book contributes in an accessible way to the growing recognition that we need to go 'back to the future' in order to progress.

Chi Kung was created in China both to promote good health and energy and to restore good health and energy when they are lacking. The exercises can be done in a gymnasium, in a dance studio, in a field, on a mountain, at work, in your home or in bed. They are both very gentle and very powerful. They may be performed at any age (including three score years and ten and beyond). They may be performed on your own, with friends, or (as in some parts of the world) in public parks in massed groups.

The Chi Kung Way: Alive with Energy will do more than explain how to begin the exercises themselves – it will also describe the fascinating social and cultural history of Chi Kung. But, while the daily practice of Chi Kung may enable you to cultivate and restore your own personal good health and energy, nothing in this world is ever completely personal. You will also require a teacher and a guide. Those encountering Chi Kung for the first time will find that this book is a guide which will last and last – though you will also need to go out and find your own personal tutor.

However this book is also a great deal more than a first-time guide to Chi Kung. This is a work which carries its learning lightly but which nevertheless brings to its pages the fruits of travel and research in America, Europe and China. Even those who have been practising Chi Kung for years will find in this small wise book insights and illuminations which will be both refreshing and new.

On a personal note, when I first met Jim over 25 years ago, American astronauts were embarking on the first moon landing. He had just completed his studies at art college; his enthusiasms were for painting, outdoor theatre, rock 'n' roll and the contemporary arts in a social setting. I had just started, as one of a team of artists, on the creation of Britain's first community arts project in a former church in city-centre Liverpool; my enthusiasms were for games, cooking Indian meals, soul music and the contemporary arts in a social setting. We worked together for the next three years – on play schemes, participatory art exhibitions, video projects and creative and co-operative games. During this period we also co-authored *The State of Play: Theatre Games as Social Art* (Great Georges Community Cultural Project, 1972).

And then our paths separated. Jim went off to study dance and acupuncture. He later brought together the arts of yesterday and today, and complementary therapies from both the East and the West, in two organizations he co-created and co-directed: the Natural Dance Workshop (in Europe) and the Evolving Institute (in America). Now he runs The Body-Energy Center with his wife Damaris Jarboux in Boulder, Colorado. It all seems a long way off from the practice of the community arts in urban areas.

And yet our paths didn't really separate at all. For James is concerned with 'doing' in the area of health through Chi Kung just as the community arts are concerned with 'doing' in the area of creative expression through participation and games. James is concerned with what is popular (available to everyone) and of quality (simply the best around). And he is passionate about communicating these concerns in a manner which is both accessible and complete.

And so after 25 years it seems that our paths are still close. We are both playing the same game, although in different arenas. Indeed, the community arts project where we first worked together ('The Blackie: An International Community Cultural Project' in Liverpool's Chinatown) now also promotes Chi Kung as a natural part of a programme embracing creativity and health, while Jim has written what is surely destined to become a definitive guide to this systematic and magical do-it-yourself energy practice. Like many people who are both 'seeking' and 'doing', the more we follow our own separate paths, the more we become closer together.

Bill Harpe, MA(Hons) Cantab.

Director of the first annual European Festival of Creative
and Co-operative Games
Great Georges Community Cultural Project,
The Blackie, Liverpool
January 1997

Chapter One

Life, Energy and Chi Kung

- Life, Energy and Chi Kung
- East and West
- Logic, Chance and Change
- The Energy System – A New Paradigm
- Our Energy Potential
- The Purpose of Practising
- The Evolution of Chi Kung
- A Guide to Practice

气 功

Chapter One

Life, Energy and Chi Kung

Chi Kung means working with our energy, developing it, cultivating it. We all know what it means to work, develop or cultivate, but what does this word 'energy' mean?

Maybe it means more than we usually assume. Maybe it is of primary importance. Maybe we should begin by taking a closer look...

Energy makes us *alive*. It is the mysterious, intangible substance that underlies how we feel, our state of health and the quality of our whole being. It is the foundation and essence of the soul and the spirit. Most people want as much energy as possible!

Energy has many forms and definitions. In the inorganic realms of physics and chemistry it ranges across the electromagnetic spectrum from thermonuclear radiation of the sun to a flashlight battery, from erupting volcanoes to catalytic conversions in a test tube. However, the energy we are talking about here is human biological energy. This could more specifically be called 'body-energy', but in this book we will simply call it 'energy'.

The word 'energy' describes the subjective experience of an internal biological process and event. However, this same experience and process may also be equally described by another familiar and greatly valued word – 'life'. It could be that in this instance 'energy' and 'life' both mean the same thing, that they both refer to the same internal biological process and experience. In this usage 'energy' is not a qualification or description of 'life', as in 'the energy of life'; neither is 'life' a qualification, a special case, of 'energy', as in the phrase 'life energy'. Here chi, 'energy' and 'life' all mean the same thing.

If we test this in normal speech then we find that the words are interchangeable:

- 'She is full of energy.' 'She is full of life.'
- 'He has no energy in him.' 'He has no life in him.'
- 'I want more energy.' 'I want more life.'
- 'They were the life of the party.' 'Their energy filled the room.'

So, if we want more life, if we want to increase and develop the life within us, then we need to increase and develop our energy. The better the energy, the better the life. When you practise Chi Kung you increase your energy, and thereby cultivate your life.

East and West

This ancient understanding of chi/energy is brand new to the West, yet has been part of the Oriental world-view for millennia. Without some sense or appreciation of this view we cannot really understand Chi Kung. Oriental cultures do not think, or experience the world, in the way that we do in the West; they have a different mind-set, different metaphors and archetypes, different paradigms and frames of reference, and different vocabularies. For instance, the highest title a practitioner can achieve in Chi Kung is to be a 'Master'. Masters are the ones people measure themselves against in the East, they are living, breathing examples of the highest accomplishment; even Emperors deferred to Masters. However, 'Master' is not a familiar Western title or usual term of address and in fact goes severely against the grain in some facets of our society. To complicate things further, there are various gradations of Master, all the way up to 'Grand Master'. At what point somebody becomes a Master is not clear, and what it means and who grants such a designation is also obscure. There are currently very few non-Asian Masters, but, as Chi Kung becomes established in the West, we will begin to see more and more people who have 'Mastered' their own energy – and they will, indeed, deserve our fullest respect.

This relates to another major issue in the East regarding Chi Kung: what 'level' a practitioner is at. Saying the word 'level' is usually accompanied by raising the forefinger of one hand and pointing towards the sky, whilst also tilting the head back slightly and looking upwards – 'This Master is very high level!' However, these levels appear almost impossible to define; it is somewhat like trying to define how well somebody plays the guitar or dances. There is a sense that, like the meaning of 'quality', it should be instinctively recognized and known. This can verge upon snobbery, but all of the higher-level practitioners and advanced teachers that I have personally met seem to have transcended such concerns themselves and are modest and exemplary human beings. A person will intuitively know a high-level practitioner – they know what they are doing and they are wonderful people.

In many ways Chi Kung is a major foundation of the 5,000-year-old Chinese culture. By understanding it we can begin to compare their civilization with ours and shed some relevant light upon our own contemporary society. The West is now coming to a new level of understanding – we are seeing and experiencing ourselves as 'energy events' rather than fixed objects. The reality of quantum physics is starting to seep into our common perception. Our understanding of what we are is changing.

Logic, Chance and Change

To make sense of Chi Kung it is also necessary to understand the system of logic underlying it; again, this is different from what has been developed in the West.

Western logic has developed from the Greek tradition, commonly known as 'Aristotlean logic'. It is a 'linear' model, based upon a *dualistic* – either/or – approach. This leads to a belief in continuous accelerating development and progress, e.g. space exploration, unlimited economic growth, everybody having everything. These rules of logic underlie not only our language, but also our way of thinking and perceiving.

Eastern logic is embedded in Oriental prehistory and is based on what is known as 'the Tao', 'the Way of Nature'. It is an 'analogue' model and based upon a *pluralistic* – and/also – approach. This leads to a belief in repeating, circular, natural cycles with slight variations – like the seasons and life-cycles common to us all.

There is all the difference in the world between these two approaches, but both are necessary for a comprehensive view. Such an integration combining linear and analogue thinking, including the core essence of both West and East, has been called by the wonderfully simple name 'analinear logic'.

Western logic is the foundation of Western science, technology, medicine and philosophy. However, in the whole of the Western scientific tradition there is no system for understanding chance, randomness or change. It is as if we are only seeing the foreground, and the background does not exist and is not relevant. This is selective vision. But recently, in the Western leading-edge science of chaos theory – which attempts to understand chance and change using the latest generations of super-computers – it is coming to be recognized that there is more than meets the eye. The background is as important as the fore-ground and it operates according to certain rules. Strangely, these rules also form the basis of the ancient Chinese classic known as the *I Ching*, 'The Book of Changes'.

It has recently been discovered – and established mathematically – that there are 64 variations in the amino acids which form the DNA molecule, the basis of all life. This is an exact match of the structure of the *I Ching*, written over 3,000 years ago, which has 64 possible variations, or chapters, relating to the full range of change. How can this be?

The *I Ching* is also based upon a mathematical range of possibilities, but one which describes the possible variations of change. The terms 'Yin' and 'Yang' describe the edges and extremes of possibilities – up and down, back and front, good and bad, male and female, order and chaos, stability and change, Heaven and Earth. It is no more possible to go beyond total Yang or total Yin than it is possible to go beyond the edges of infinity. Between them lie the range of all possible conditions and states, and these states interact and can change into each other. Yin and Yang are the book-ends of reality.

In this system there are eight stages of change between full Yang and full Yin. There are two levels on which this operates – Heaven and Earth – which interact together such that $8 \times 8 = 64$, giving the number of chapters in the *I Ching*. This system of logic seems to accurately describe and reflect what is actually going on between Heaven and Earth, and how everything does, indeed, work.

To include this Yin/Yang system of logic into our way of thinking and perceiving can align us more closely with our own true nature and the true nature of reality.

The Energy System – A New Paradigm

Part of our own nature is our energy system. The idea that the human body has an energy system is now becoming generally accepted throughout the West, thanks to the spread of such long-established Eastern arts as acupuncture, Oriental medicine and the exercise practices of Tai Chi/shadow boxing. Thirty years ago, for instance, acupuncture was rare in our society; now it has become mainstream. When I moved from England to Boulder, Colorado (a small city of 90,000 people in the Rocky Mountains), in the early 1980s, I was the only registered acupuncturist. Now, 15 years later, there are 67 practitioners in town! Drawn upon a graph this is almost a vertical line upwards. But this is not unique – similar stories are happening everywhere.

The energy system is as much a part of our anatomy and physiology as the nervous system, circulatory system, skeletal system, muscular system and all of the other anatomical systems that, in total, make us what we are. While this understanding is the very foundation of Oriental medicine, it is not part of the Western medical model. However, this may be very different in the not too distant future – acupuncture is now being included in the curricula of some Western medical schools, and Chi Kung is beginning to be used and taught in hospitals.

What exactly is the energy system? It is of a different order than the material, physical, reality that we can touch and see – it is the next level up the hierarchy of functions. It is a 'control system' for everything else – all of the organs, tissues, endocrine glands, sense organs, emotions, mental capacities and even what we call the 'spirit'.

Chi Kung teaches a person how to 'control the control system' through a wide range of practices and exercises. It is a profound form of self-regulation. If a person does not know how to control their own system, then they are in turn controlled, and limited, by it. They are, quite literally, 'out of control'. So, Chi Kung is a highly developed science of self-control, in the best possible sense. It teaches us how to take care of ourselves.

Our Energy Potential

According to Chi Kung, the energy system has a specific anatomy and physiology. This can be also understood as its *structure* – what it is – and its *function* – how it works. This is as precise a science as Western anatomy and physiology, it is just not familiar in our everyday Western culture.

When a person says that they are 'tired', they 'don't have enough energy' or they feel 'lifeless' they are, in one way or another, making a statement about the condition and state of their chi.

One of the problems is that there are no easy or common words in our language to describe this. It is all said in vague generalities and with a sense that there is nothing that can be done to change or improve such a state except to rest and recuperate. Indeed, rest, sleep and relaxation will generally improve the state of a person's energy – not doing anything for a time, not expending energy in activity, allows the body and energy system to re-establish a state of equilibrium. Everything balances out again and the person is ready for the next round. The body has an in-built ability to return to the neutral state. We sleep for eight hours out of every 24, one third of our lives, and that allows this rebalancing and recharging process to take place automatically and unconsciously. However, in Chi Kung there are many ways of improving the energy consciously and intentionally. That is its major purpose and function.

A useful analogy would be with a battery. A battery is a means of storing energy. Some batteries can just manage to get a small bulb to dimly flicker, others can start diesel train engines. The more energy used up by a battery the less will be left – simple physics. It is then necessary to recharge it from an outside source. Chi Kung is a way to increase the size of the human battery and consciously to charge it to its full capacity. It is a way to maximize energy potential.

There are four major components involved in energy development and control: 1) physical postures and movements, 2) the meridian energy system, 3) mental concentration and 4) breathing patterns:

1 The physical body can be put into a wide variety of postures and moved in a range of patterns. Some of these are geometric shapes or configurations which 'drive' the energy in particular ways and which can create energy 'feedback loops'. The longer a person stays in a particular posture or performs a set of movements, the stronger the energy gets.

2 The Oriental energy system, as mentioned earlier, is a precise anatomical system of pathways and connections. Just as there are certain muscles in particular places, which function in very specific ways, there are particular energy pathways, known as meridians, which have very specific functions. In order to perform Chi Kung consciously it is necessary to understand what these pathways are, what they connect to, what their functions are and how they all relate together. This is, in effect, technical training – it has to be learned and memorized and understood, just as it is necessary to understand the muscular system to do effective massage.

3 Mental concentration involves using the conscious mind and will-power. One of the primary principles of Chi Kung is that *the mind* leads *the energy*. Where the mind leads, the energy will follow. However, this requires specific training and discipline in order for it to happen

effectively. It is as if the mind has to 'grab hold' of the energy and make it move in the ways that it wants. This is not just vague wishful thinking – it is very specific and focused. Chi Kung trains a person how to do it.

4 Breathing patterns can be consciously directed and performed in a variety of ways to increase the depth and power of the energy – normal breathing, reverse breathing, stop/start breathing, holding the breath, counting the breaths and so on. Breathing is one of the two ways of bringing external energy into the system – it is known as 'the energy of Heaven'. The other, of course, is eating, known as 'the energy of Earth'.

These components – the body, energy, mind and breathing – are co-ordinated and integrated in performing Chi Kung.

The Purpose of Practising

Chi Kung, as already mentioned, is a means to increase the volume and heighten the frequency of body-energy, and to put it under conscious control. It is a way to bring the chi into its best state, so that everything functions the way it is intended to, and thereby to get all of the various aspects of a person's being – the internal organs, tissues, endocrine glands, sense organs, emotions, mental capacities and spirit – operating in a co-ordinated and harmonious whole. In the Oriental view this is the condition of health – when a person's energy has the right balance (between left and right, front and back, inside and outside and up and down), when it is flowing freely without blockages or obstructions, when it has the right quality and good volume. If any of these parameters is not correct there will be a corresponding level of dysfunction, which can manifest from 'not quite feeling up to par' all the way to severe physical, emotional or mental symptoms. The more out of order the energy is, the greater will be the problems.

In the West we do not have a complete and accurate model of what we are, because the energy system is not part of our medical model. But trying to understand the human being without including the energy system is like trying to understand the local weather without satellite images of global weather patterns. The energy system is the co-ordinating and integrating control system which ties the human organism together and makes it all work. In the Oriental model, *what* we are and *how* we work is as important as *who* we are. Emotions are seen as manifestations of the energy patterns. If a person is angry or frustrated, it may be a manifestation of congestion of the energy in the liver and gall bladder. If someone is anxious or feeling overwhelmed, it may be the result of uncontrolled energy in the heart. If a person is sad or longing, it may just as well be because of weakness and emptiness of the energy in the lungs and colon as for any emotional or external reason.

If the energy system is operating correctly, if it is balanced and free-flowing with the right quality and good volume, then the emotions will be fully available and appropriate to the particular situation. If the energy is stuck, blocked, empty, weak, excessive, stagnant or otherwise out of order in any area, there will be corresponding disturbances and imbalances in the feelings and attitudes. So just concentrating on getting the energy working correctly can often take care of emotional problems. This approach focuses on the condition of the energy right now, rather than looking for reasons in the past or future. This is one of the great values of Chi Kung – a person can put themselves right, and feel at their best, through just getting their energy working correctly. The personal and social value of this is incalculable.

The Evolution of Chi Kung

The origin of Chi Kung is clouded in antiquity. There is no commonly agreed chronology or exact line of development – that still remains to be pieced together. It has come down through the centuries in fragments in the form of relics, legends and books. It has also been passed on through more than 100 generations by word-of-mouth and personal instruction – obviously a method of transmission that can lead to an infinite variety of permutations and distortions. Written records were not easily accessible or reliable, however, because they were often cloaked in esoteric and symbolic language whose very purpose was to keep the information secret. So it was not widely disseminated.

Chi Kung was held a closely guarded secret by its practitioners for both good and not so good reasons. The good reasons concerned the strength of Chi Kung. It is extraordinarily powerful and needs to be learnt and practised correctly or there can be a whole array of detrimental effects. This aspect could become a problem as Chi Kung enters the West because there are currently no standards or controls in place and the free-for-all, entrepreneurial spirit of Westerners will undoubtedly result in all manner of variations, including incomplete training and partial, dislocated practices. However, standards of reference will, no doubt, emerge before too long.

The not-so-good reasons for secrecy were the personal self-interest of the teachers. The knowledge and practices were, in essence, sold to students, so that the teachers had a very strong vested interest in keeping the students studying with them, rather than learning all of the practices then setting themselves up teaching in competition. This dimension is regrettable, but understandable when a teacher's livelihood, and the welfare of their family, was involved.

A further complication was that teachers would hold on to the information, sometimes not even transmitting it to their own children or most committed disciples. Sometimes teachers died without passing information on. A father might teach a special technique or variation to his son as a birthday gift, but Chi Kung was rarely taught to the female children because once a woman married, what she knew belonged to her husband's family and she was obliged to share everything with them. Because of this cultural tradition there are few prominent female Chi Kung practitioners in Chinese history.

Various forms have, however, been passed down and have withstood the test of time, for the simple fact that they work. Such practices as the Five Animal Frolics, the Eight Pieces of Brocade, Iron Shirt Chi Kung, Bone Marrow Washing, the various styles of Tai Chi Chuan, the Six Healing Sounds and the Microcosmic Orbit have come through as complete practice sets, although each of these now has a wide variety of permutations. There are also a range of practices of more recent origin, such as Wild Goose Chi Kung, Soaring Crane Chi Kung, Swimming Dragon Chi Kung and others which have been created by individual practitioners.

The question arises of what is the common basis of all of these styles and forms. What they all share is their foundation in the primary anatomy and physiology of the energy system – the 12 major organ meridians and the eight extra meridians. These energy structures are the root of all of the various forms because they are the anatomical basis that everything operates from and which everybody has. Just as a guitar has a body, a neck and six strings, but an infinite variety of music can be played upon it, so the forms of Chi Kung are variations of how to play the instrument of these 20 major meridians.

Also, learning the anatomy and physiology of the eight extra meridians provides a solid foundation for all forms of practice, just as learning Latin and Greek provides the basis for understanding all Western languages. There is common agreement among practitioners that learning these practices is a basic requirement. It may well turn out that 'Eight Extra Meridian Chi Kung' is the 'core curriculum' for all further training.

Up until the mid 1950s there were a large number of different long-established styles, forms, traditions and approaches for working with energy, which included practices with such names as Nei Dan, Wei Dan, Dao Yin, Tai Chi, Kung Fu, Wu Shu, Tu Na and Tugu Naxin. There were Taoist, Buddhist, Confucian and Tibetan forms which had all intermixed over time.

In 1955 the Chinese Government wanted to make clear the answer to the question 'What is *chi*?' So Chi Kung was invented in 1955 by a Chinese Communist Government sub-committee ... or at least the name was! A research group, which included Master Gui Zhen Liu and other Masters, was instructed to look into the practice. After much discussion and consideration they took the word *kung* from Kung Fu (the martial art), which can be interpreted as meaning 'work/developing/cultivating', and added it to *chi* to create the totally new term 'Chi Kung'. In one way or another, the earlier forms were incorporated into the new all-encompassing concept. So, Chi Kung is a modern amalgam of many ancient theories and practices – which means that it is not one thing in particular, but many, many things, all interwoven. It is an umbrella term which could be compared to the recent Western term 'holistic health'.

By comparison, a similar event occurred at about the same time, when another Government group was involved in modernizing Chinese medicine, primarily acupuncture and herbs. They took the body of knowledge that had accumulated since antiquity and modified it to align with the principles and politics of the current Communist dynasty. This became known as 'traditional Chinese medicine', abbreviated as TCM.

This is obviously somewhat of a misnomer. It bears little resemblance to the traditional Taoist styles of medical practice, but is now what is taught in medical schools in China, and has therefore become the predominant style taught and practised in the West.

It is worthy of note that in the confusion of cross-cultural translation and the chance elements of historical transmission, the Chinese began using a Western term for one of their own ancient and unique practices – acupuncture. The Government published official books with titles such as *Essentials of Chinese Acupuncture* and *An Outline of Chinese Acupuncture*. The Chinese words for what the West knows as acupuncture are Zhen Jou – two separate words which directly translate as 'needle' and 'heat'. In this sense it is a verb, not a noun. It is an action that is performed and done in order to treat a person's energy. Strangely, nobody I have ever spoken to, or any meeting of acupuncturists I have attended, knows where the word 'acupuncture' comes from or who first used it (maybe it was Marco Polo himself) – yet there are now in the region of 20,000 acupuncturists practising in the West! Who invented this word which is now so important to so many people, including all the patients who get treated? If you know, please tell me!

When looking at anything Chinese it is a good idea to ask if it is pre- or post-Communist. Was it practised in this way before 1949? The Chinese Government has many questions to answer... However, on with the story of Chi Kung. In 1957, just two years after being officially sanctioned, all research and public teaching of Chi Kung abruptly stopped as the whole country was propelled into the Great Leap Forward by Chairman Mao Ze Dong. This then led into the catastrophic Cultural Revolution from 1966 to 1976, which plunged the country into unprecedented upheaval and turmoil.

In 1980, when political stability had been restored, it again became permissible to research and teach Chi Kung. Indeed, from '80 to '89 there was a veritable 'Chi Kung craze'. With the new freedoms, all manner of Masters and teachers, at every level, appeared. Every kind of Chi Kung was taught. Books were written and were made easily available. After years of repression people flocked to it by the millions – it was, after all, their old ancient traditions in a new form. Some of the teachers were more 'business Masters' than Chi Kung Masters and large sums of money were made. There was also a down side – some people suffered injury from 'Chi Kung deviation', that is, wrong or incompetent instruction. A handful of Masters were famous enough to fill sports stadia (similar, perhaps, to the well known Western evangelist Billy Graham) where they created chi fields, and conducted mass healings of people. The authorities began to pay attention.

In 1989 the Pro-Democracy movement initiated the demonstrations in Tian An Men Square, watched by the whole world on TV. Powerful Chi Kung Masters turned up and emitted their chi to the massed crowds, thereby becoming engaged in the politics of it all. After the tragic ending of the demonstration, Chi Kung was blamed as one of the underlying causes of the social unrest. So since that time the Government has maintained strict control of the practice. In order now to teach publicly, in one of the large parks where people gather every morning, it is necessary to get a permit in advance and to have the programme approved and monitored by the authorities. Obviously this is not a situation very conducive to higher level practices or innovation. Now, it is the Government-sponsored and supported teachers and researchers who become famous. Small groups still gather around individual Masters, but there is not much cross-fertilization or collaboration.

However, scientific research into Chi Kung is being conducted in universities and clinics throughout the East, and industry too is funding programmes. An article in the American journal *Business Week* (January 1995) reported that in Japan senior executives of major companies such as Sony, Mitsubishi Electric, NEC and Casio Computers are training with '*Ki* Masters'. They say that it increases their vitality and efficiency, and consequently their profit margins. It keeps them young. One executive stated, 'I think *Ki* treatment has helped me grow this company from $70 million a year to $600 million.' Japan's Ministry of International Trade & Industry has formed a committee to look into practical uses of *Ki* energy. More than 10 major companies are funding research at Tokyo's University of Electro-Communications.

All over Asia conferences are taking place where doctors, clinicians, researchers, teachers and practitioners are gathering to report on their studies and exchange information. The World Academic Society of Medical Qigong, based in Beijing and the largest organization in China, hosts international conferences. In 1993, when I attended one with my wife Damaris, more than 500 medical professionals and Chi Kung practitioners from over a dozen countries – including China, Korea, Taiwan, Japan, Malaysia, Australia, Sweden, Italy, France, Britain, the United States and Canada – heard 105 papers presented on such topics as:

- 'Spectrum Analysis Effect of the Emitted *Chi* on EEGs of Normal Subjects'
- 'Clinical Observations on 30 Cases of Cancer Treated by Chi Kung Therapy'
- 'The Clinical Report on 75 Cases of Chronic Hepatitis B Treated by Chi Kung'
- 'Observations on Effects of 31 Cases of Diabetes Treated by Huichugong'
- 'Chi Kung's Curative Effect on Lumbago and Joint Pain'

Obviously, this is serious scientific medical research, and it is ever-increasing, as more and more studies are conducted and the dialogue and exchange develop.

Some of the technical research has resulted in the creation of instruments which replicate the effects of Chi Kung healers and which are now used widely in clinical settings and treatment.

One remarkable research programme is being conducted by a doctor of both Chinese traditional and Western medicine who is also a Chi Kung Master – Wan, Su-Jian, MD. He is a Colonel in the Chinese Army and has created the Army Qigong Hospital, which also serves as a school for children aged 11 to 18, where gifted children from around the country are trained in Chi Kung healing and upon graduation are assigned to various hospitals and clinics around the country. Dr Wan's speciality is paralysis. He was one of the rescue team following a devastating earthquake in northern China and was in a building with two other soldiers when it collapsed on them, trapping them inside. He lay in the darkness, unable to move. The other two rescuers panicked and were overwhelmed by their fear, screaming, shouting and crying for help. Wan quietly lay in the darkness and practised Chi Kung, circulating his *chi* and conserving his energy. When they were finally uncovered he was the only one alive. He found that he was able to help many cases of paralysis suffered in the earthquake by applying his form of Chi Kung and, with the blessing and support of the Government, established his school to train young practitioners.

Another recent development in China is the creation of Chi Kung resorts, similar to health farms in the West, which are privately run. These are residential settings where people can stay and undergo intensive Chi Kung therapy and training, along with other forms of traditional Chinese medicine. They offer the opportunity for in-depth training and are proving to be very popular. A parallel development is taking place in the West, as teachers are realizing that such settings provide an appropriate context for people to learn and develop in-depth practice skills away from the hurly-burly of normal everyday life. Once such skills are embodied they can then be applied as needed.

But, by one of those peculiar and unpredictable quantum leaps of history, the Chi Kung craze has jumped across the cultural tracks and is now being hungrily picked up by the West, where there are no Government controls and where there is instant dissemination of information. Now it is spreading at an accelerating rate. It will, no doubt, prove to be as impossible to control as rock 'n' roll! In the West there are now in fact Chi Kung groupies, including middle-aged and balding males, who flock around the latest Chi Kung Master just as they would with a rock star. People will spend all their money, drive for miles, camp overnight and wait for hours, all to 'get the *chi*'!

Camping and waiting are not necessary, of course. The book you are now reading is saving you an immense amount of physical discomfort and expense!

A Guide to Practice

This book will give you an experience of your own energy through Chi Kung. It contains four chapters of exercises and practices. There are numerous physical benefits and effects to these, including the regulation of blood pressure, body temperature, sleep cycles, appetite, digestion, peristalsis and other primary functions. The exercises have been gathered from various sources and from my teaching experience, and modified,

adapted and designed to be able to be done by anybody in average health – whatever their previous experience. They are
simple and easy to do, but very effective. They are intended to
be useful at any time, as, and when, they are needed – but first
you have to learn them.

How to Learn

The way in which someone learns how their energy feels is by first
doing a particular practice and then paying attention to the effect,
thereby getting the feedback. In this way you will build up an energy
language vocabulary and will slowly create your own internal library
of memories of experiences (a proposal for an energy language is
presented in an appendix at the back of the book, *see* p.211). Doing
the practices, feeling the sensations and remembering and record-
ing them is the best way to learn. It requires a passive and receptive
attitude of mind.

Progressive Development

Each of the four chapters is organized somewhat progressively, and
initially it is best to start from the beginning and work your way
through them. Also, each chapter moves on to the next.
However, once you have learned the practices you can choose
to do any one independently. If you start at the beginning and

develop slowly, you will gradually acquire greater and more refined skills and abilities.

The Number of Repetitions

At various places there are instructions for the number of times to do a particular practice – the number of repetitions. These are not fixed, just general guidelines. Practices can be done for differing numbers of times. In any individual treatment the number of repetitions would be specific to the particular person. As a general indication it is usual to do groups of odd numbers – 3, 9, 15, 25 – although repetitions of 6, 12 and 36 are common. Pay attention to yourself and feel the right number of repetitions for you.

Breathing

There are many forms of breathing techniques employed in Taoist practices for specific purposes, but these are too elaborate and extensive to go into here. However, breathing is a valuable way of counting and controlling the amount of time you spend at a particular point or area of the body, especially if you have your eyes closed. As a general rule, unless otherwise indicated, begin by breathing in and out three times at each point. Later you can vary the number of breaths – 6, 9, 15 or more times –

and therefore spend more time at each point. In the early stages of practice it is advised to be consistent with the number of breaths in any given practice. When you have developed some level of sensitivity and skill, you will find that you may want to spend more time at one point and less at another. At that stage follow your intuition and inner guidance.

———————————

The following are some additional guidelines and notes. They are meant as general indications for how to proceed.

- To begin, read through the instructions thoroughly. Then try the exercises out, repeating them slowly and gently at first until you get the general idea and intention. Then try them on your own without referring to the instructions.

- Because of the inherent difficulty involved in reading instructions whilst simultaneously practising it may be helpful if you begin by having somebody else read them out to you as you practise, or try taping the instructions, then playing them back to guide you. A boxed set of audiotapes of these practices is available, *see* Further Information, p. 219.

- In places various words are used to mean the same thing. For example, 'mind', 'attention', 'awareness' and 'energy' are used interchangeably at times. In these cases pay attention to the general sense and meaning.

• Check yourself out first. See what state your mind and energy are in. Do the practice, then see what changes it produces and how it makes you feel. Do you get clearer, lighter, fresher, calmer, brighter, stronger...?

• Learn from your own experience. If a practice doesn't feel right or if you get any adverse reaction, slow down, don't do it so hard or so long, or discontinue. Try again another time. Persevere. Continue until you feel it is right.

• Take these exercises as general guidelines. Don't get stuck with following a rigid form. Understand the basic principles and develop from there, using common sense. Experiment.

Dos

Wear comfortable, loose-fitting clothes, with nothing binding at the waist. Practise in the early morning, if possible. Practise where you won't be disturbed or distracted. Turn off the phone. Practise outdoors if you are able to. Set time aside. Relieve nature before beginning. If in doubt, bring your energy to your navel. Eat properly and get enough rest. Live a moderate lifestyle. Do it until you get the flow of your chi. Practise as often as you can.

Don'ts

Don't practise immediately before or after a meal. Don't overeat. Don't practise if emotionally upset. Don't overdo it if you are ill or greatly fatigued – rest first. Don't overindulge in sex. Don't expose yourself to adverse climates – excess heat, cold, wind, damp or dryness – or extreme weather conditions. Don't worry, be happy!

———————————

If you begin by practising conscientiously, so that you develop the feel, knack and skill of the practices, then you will find that you start to do them automatically and naturally. Once you have achieved this, then integrate them into your daily routine. Work with them. Play with them. Try them different ways. See what works for you, and use it to your own best advantage.

Chi Kung is an adventure into yourself. Take the time to learn these practices and they will be yours for life. They may end up being some of your most important and valued possessions – a collection of gems and treasures.

Chapter Two

Natural Chi Kung

气 功

Chapter Two

Natural Chi Kung

We already do Chi Kung in everyday life. We are already Chi Kung practitioners.

It is how we naturally work.
It is instinctive and spontaneous.
It is Natural Chi Kung – natural energy cultivation.

Walking down the street can be Chi Kung. Working can be Chi Kung. Cleaning the house can be Chi Kung. Gardening can be Chi Kung. Watching TV can be Chi Kung. Shopping can be Chi Kung. Eating, drinking and breathing can be Chi Kung. It all depends on *how* we actually do something.

Many of our unconscious actions and activities do instinctively work to affect, improve and conserve our energy, but other activities use it up and waste it. Some activities are energy recharging, others are energy depleting. Some natural movements and postures are Chi Kung; most are not.

Questions to ask yourself are: '*How* am I doing what I am doing, and *how* should I best do it to accumulate, conserve and preserve my energy?' 'What activities naturally and instinctively gather or develop my energy and which ones waste it?' 'What is the balance between Yin and Yang, rest and activity, discharging and recharging?'

Natural Chi Kung We Already Do

There are natural postures and movements that all people unconsciously assume or perform. Some of these relate to specific body locations which are energy centres; some are areas related to particular meridian energy lines; some are positions our body naturally takes; some are in relation to the external energy of other people, living things, inanimate objects and the atmosphere. These instinctive actions could all be called Natural Chi Kung. For example:

- There are certain positions of the hands in relationship to each other which generate energy – such as clasping them together in the lap or rubbing them to make them warm.

- There are areas which are specific points and energy centres, which we unconsciously affect with our hands and unknowingly use to bring energy to a particular area when needed – such as holding the forehead to clear the mind or brushing the fingers back over the head.

- There are actions which can accumulate, build, develop and preserve energy – such as stretching overhead and breathing in deeply, or lying down to rest.

- There are spontaneous self-massage actions and activities that stimulate and affect energy in a particular meridian, area or organ – such as rubbing an aching stomach or massaging the eyes.

The Power in the Palms

The centres of the palms are major energy points, called Lao Gong (the Palace of Weariness). They emit extraordinary energy. It has been found through scientific research in China that the palms emit a combination of infrasonic, electromagnetic, microwave and infrared wavelengths. This is the 'healing energy' emitted by Chi Kung healers. It is also the energy used in all other forms of energy healing. Use of the hands can greatly influence a person's energy.

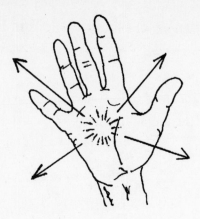

The Lao Gong point

There are many hand positions that act to accumulate, recharge, balance, seal in, disperse or drain energy. Everybody does them, often unknowingly.

For example, there are four common positions of placing the palms in relation to each other to seal energy in or to increase it:

- *Clasping palms together*: Clasping the palms together, fingers curled around the sides and back of the other hand. This seals energy in.

- *Interlocking fingers*: Interlocking the fingers, bringing the palms into close proximity and thereby also sealing them.

- *Fingertips touching*: Just touching the fingertips together, forming a 'church steeple', sometimes palms touching, sometimes not.

• *Rubbing the hands together*: Rubbing the palms together, to make them warm or as an expression of emotion, stimulates and generates energy.

There are other common things that everybody does, without any idea of why they are doing them. Some of these may be familiar:

Hands over the Lower Abdomen

This is perhaps the most common and usual posture. It is also the most powerful and important. People take this position when they are at ease on their feet; it is a very comfortable position and can be maintained for a long time. People also often hold their hands over this point when they are sitting or place their hands over this point when lying down. Here the hands cover the Lower Tan Tien, the power centre of the body, thereby retaining energy and also recharging it in the system.

Cross Palms Behind the Back of the Head

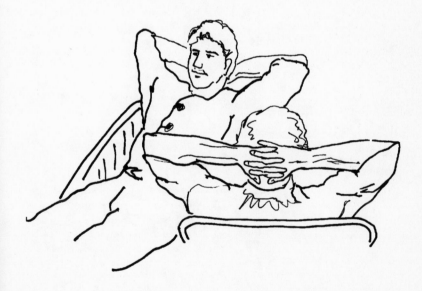

This is one of the most common positions for relaxation. People do it all over the planet. However, they rarely suspect that the point at the back of the skull, slightly off to either side of the centre line and naturally covered by the centre of each palm when the fingers are interlaced, is an energy point called Bladder 9 (the Jade Pillow). This relates to the cerebellum, the lower brain which controls breathing, heartbeat and various other functions of the autonomic nervous system. Placing the palms in this position brings their healing energy to feed, calm, relax and regulate the cerebellum and lower brain, and therefore many of the automatic body functions. It is like pressing the 'reset' button.

Hands on Top of Head

It is common to see people placing their interlaced fingers and palms on the point on the top of their head. This is one of the major Chi Kung points – Governor 20 (Bai Hui/the Meeting of the Hundred). It is a way to seal the energy in. It is the crown point. It feeds into the pineal gland, and thereby stimulates the brain, consciousness and awareness. In Taoism this point is said to be the place where the spirit enters and leaves the body.

Joining the Front and Back Channels

In periods where concentration is called for – as in a lecture, meeting or negotiation – people often join their hands and fingertips in a 'church steeple' position, and cover their nose and mouth. This is the major area of connection between the front and the back channels – the Governor and Conception meridians. It is a primary way of maintaining energy. In Chi Kung practice this is accomplished by simply touching the tip of the tongue to the roof of the mouth, just behind the teeth. And, of course, nobody will have the faintest idea that a person is doing it.

S-t-r-e-t-c-h-i-n-g

A common movement performed to s-t-r-e-t-c-h, and thereby release tension and congestion, is to raise the hands overhead, palms facing upwards. Sometimes the fingers are interlaced. This is often accompanied by a sigh or sound. These positions are used in Taoist practice to cleanse the body of stale energy, especially that of the lungs, heart and liver. This posture is also used to gather, through the palms, the fresh energy of Heaven – the atmosphere, sky, sun, moon and stars.

Touching

Touching is a usual activity for everybody. A person gently touches children, as a sign of care and attention, to soothe or reassure. They touch a spouse or lover with affection and hold hands (join their energy together through the Lao Gong point) while sitting or walking together. They shake hands with somebody and instantly get the 'feel' of them. They stroke pets, and the pets like it. Touching other living beings with the palms is a major way of connecting with, and exchanging, energy. It is the basis of Chi Kung healing and its Western equivalents known as healing touch, therapeutic touch and so on. Stones, trees, earth, gems, crystals and flowers all have their own energy and touching can be a way of drawing their energy into ourselves. Next time you find yourself touching somebody or something, stop and consider why ... and pay attention to how it feels.

Normal Everyday Life

There are generally three basic positions the body can be in in normal everyday life – standing, sitting or lying. Gymnasts, mountain climbers and astronauts have a different relationship to gravity, but normally these are the three primary possibilities. Each has its own advantages and its own limitations when practising Chi Kung. The appropriate positions for the practices in this book are indicated accordingly.

Sitting

People in our contemporary culture spend a lot of their time sitting. This involves staying in a fixed body position sitting on the buttocks for extended periods of time. There are limited possibilities of arm and leg movements. Some people sit in a good alignment and posture, with the head balanced over the bowl of the pelvis, knees shoulder-width apart bent at right angles and with the feet flat on the floor. This position allows the energy to flow most freely and can be maintained for extended periods of time. It is the desired posture for practising Chi Kung when sitting.

Walking

Walking is the preferred and usual human moving experience. Everybody walks (unless physically unable to). One of the all-time favourite human activities is going for a walk outdoors in nature. When a person walks in the natural environment the energy field which extends outside and around the body is cleansed by the atmosphere, plants and trees ... and they feel 're-freshed', freshened up.

Connect with the earth when you walk. As you lift off the ground draw the energy of the earth into you, through the point called Yong Quan (Bubbling Spring) on the soles of your feet, in the centre just behind the toes. This is the equivalent of the Lao Gong point in the centre of the palms.

Lying

Lying places a person in a passive, horizontal relationship to gravity. This could be called 'Horizontal Chi Kung'. When lying down you can 'let go' and everything can relax. It uses almost no muscular effort. Voluntary and involuntary muscular controls are turned off. The normal person spends something in the region of eight hours out of every 24, one third of life, lying down while sleeping; this allows the body to go into automatic recharge and the energy system to rebalance itself. Sleep equalizes our energy.

Sleeping with Another Person

When somebody sleeps next to another person their major energy centres are aligned and they lie in each other's energy field. A couple lying next to each other on a continual basis for many years will tend to compensate and adapt to each other's field, even though these may not individually be operating correctly. Join them together and they create their own complete whole (although this whole may not be ideally balanced). This is one of the reasons for the tremendous impact felt in the loss of a spouse or partner – the other person's energy is no longer there to complete the whole. Both halves of a couple have a strong obligation and responsibility to their partner to stay in the best energy state possible.

Other common movements include bouncing, shaking, swinging, twisting, running, jumping and many more. A person can do these movements just for the fun of it, pay attention to what the movements do to their energy and then add that awareness to their personal energy-memory library!

Chi Kung is also part of recreation, sports and dance. These activities have a direct and immediate effect on the whole energy system, which is sometimes the underlying reason why people do them – it puts their energy right and makes them feel better.

The various postures and movements a person makes are very important to what happens to their energy during everyday activities. Being conscious of this will allow a person to have choice and control over their energy.

Consider: What is the effect of the action somebody is doing? What activities and positions block, congest or deplete energy? Which activities increase and develop energy?

Take an activity and work with it. Play with it. Try it different ways. See what works and use it to the best advantage.

So, Naturally...

Remember, Chi Kung is natural. There are many ways in which every person already does it. The Orient didn't invent body-energy – it is an inherent part of our biological being. Just because nobody told us it existed or because the orthodox medical profession knows nothing about it does not mean it has not been part of us from the moment of conception. It has always been there. It is an essential foundation of how we function. It is the essence of our life. Indeed, in some ways it is the very 'stuff of life' – our energy is life itself.

People instinctively do things to work with their energy – to rebalance it, to replenish it when it is low, to disperse it when it is congested, to free it when it is stuck, to exchange and share it with others, to enrich it, to enjoy and to celebrate it. People do all of this naturally and instinctively, because this is how we work. It is, at the deepest level, what we are. So why not take this energy that we already have, develop it, cultivate it, increase it and use it to feel our best?

Chapter Three

How It Works

- The Foundations of Chi Kung
- Eastern and Western Medicine
- The Tao
- Structure
- Function
- External Energy and Natural Cycles
- What to Avoid
- Summary

气 功

Chapter Three

How It Works

The Foundations of Chi Kung

The energy system is as real as the muscular system, the circulatory system, the nervous system and all of the other physical systems. It is a primary biological function. It is the foundation of Oriental medicine and culture, but it is hardly even known about in the West. Strange indeed! It is as if we used money, but never learned to count, had books but never learned to read. Understanding our energy and how it works is a more primary, basic and important skill than knowing how to count or read, and yet there has been almost no way available to learn it. Now there is Chi Kung!

To understand Chi Kung more fully and learn how it works it is necessary first to understand some basic principles. This chapter lays down the foundation.

Eastern and Western Medicine

Western medicine is based upon Western science and Eastern medicine upon Eastern science. There are large differences between these two sciences.

Western science is the basis of Western technology. It is a rational, objective, logical, reductionist, left-brain view of the world; in China this would be called a 'Yang' point of view. It has obviously brought great benefits to humankind; however, it also has many detrimental consequences, as clearly seen in our environmental and social problems. Western medicine is based on this science and so there are problems, as well as benefits, with the way it is practised.

Eastern science is based on a different understanding of what science is and operates according to different laws and principles. It requires using an intuitive, artistic, metaphorical, holistic, right-brain approach; this would be called a 'Yin' point of view. Understanding Eastern science and philosophy amounts to asking Westerners to change the way they think about the world and how it works. It is a radical proposal. But although this science is largely foreign to us, it is as valid as our own. Oriental medicine, which has provided first-class health care for a quarter of the world's population for the whole of recorded history, is based on this science.

Despite their different approaches, Eastern and Western science do complement each other. Combining the two is an inclusion and an addition – it does not take away anything, but rather adds to what we already know. In many ways the East needs and wants what we have – technology and its comforts – and we need and want what they have – a profound under-standing of body-energy and how it underlies our health and state of being. In China many doctors are already trained in *both* traditional Chinese medicine *and* Western medicine. Through Chi Kung, we may be about to enter into a new period of human history where the most profound knowledge of both East and West is integrated. This could be described as 'joining Yin and Yang'.

The Tao

Chinese science is largely based on a view of the universe which is known as 'the Tao' (pronounced 'Dow' in English). It essentially means 'nature'. The ancient Taoists, like the ancient Greeks, were early scientists – they observed nature and its workings. The best translation of the Tao is 'the Way' – the way in which nature works. Hence the title of this book

The Tao is considered to be the original source and underlying basis of everything that exists. It is the Great Mystery, the Truth. It permeates everything that is. It is said to be unnameable, indescribable and ineffable. Our highest possible achievement is to understand it correctly and align ourselves with it; this is known as 'being in the Tao'. To achieve this is said 'to attain the Tao', which is what all Taoists aspire to. This state of being is beyond thought. The ancient Chinese philosopher known as Lao Tzu (Old Master) first outlined the principles of the Tao in the book *Tao Te Ching* (fifth century BC), which translates as 'The Book of the Way and its Virtue' and is widely acclaimed as one of the greatest classics of human thought. Although there are specialized forms of Buddhist, Tibetan and other styles of Chi Kung, Taoism is its main foundation.

There are two distinct branches of Taoism – one is philosophical, the other is religious. Philosophical Taoism, like Western science, is non-theistic: it does not need to address or question whether there is, or is not, a God. It is essentially a philosophy which looks at the way things work and how we can best align ourselves with it. It is practical, common-sense and down-to-earth. Religious Taoism grew out of ancient

Chinese folk religion, and has its own pantheon of gods and immortals, heaven and hell, canons and priests and so on, as all religions do. In most ways it is completely separate and distinct from the philosophy of Taoism and need be of no concern to us now; it is the philosophy of Taoism that we are concerned with here. Understanding, believing and accepting philosophical Taoism is independent of any religious beliefs – you can be a Christian and a Taoist, a Muslim and a Taoist or an atheist and a Taoist. The main laws and principles of Taoism which concern us are known as Yin and Yang, the Five Elements, the Eight Diagrams and Wu Wei.

Yin and Yang

Everything has an opposite – up/down, hot/cold, dark/light, positive/negative, male/female, and so on. These opposites, as already mentioned, are known as Yin and Yang. This basic polarity is inherent in the nature of reality, and is also part of the architecture of our brains and minds. It is the 'binary code', represented by 0 and 1, in mathematics, which makes possible much of our electronic technology. Yin and Yang operate according to very specific laws. These include the principles: everything has a Yin and a Yang aspect; everything has a proportion of Yin and Yang; every Yin and Yang can be further divided; Yin and Yang create each other; Yin and Yang control each other; and Yin and Yang can each transform into the other.

Yin and Yang are represented by the now familiar symbol, which is known as the Tai Qi – the Supreme Ultimate. Graphically they are represented by a broken or an unbroken line.

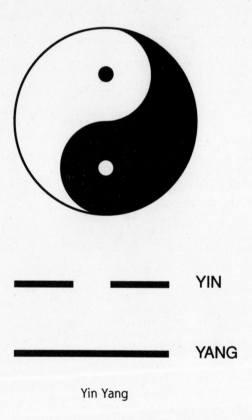

YIN

YANG

Yin Yang

The Five Elements

After the primary division into Yin and Yang the universe is understood to consist of what are called 'the Five Elements' or 'the Five Phases'. These are known as wood, fire, earth, metal and water. This is a way of describing things and situations according to their basic inherent qualities.

The Five Elements/Phases are primarily based upon the seasons, and the qualities and characteristics of each Element in terms of the 'energetics' of that particular season. The seasons, in turn, are based upon the energetics of the rotation of the Earth around the sun, the tilt of the Earth's axis, and the gravitational pull of the moon. So, the Five Elements/Phases are fundamentally based upon the sun, Earth and moon cycles. More about this later.

The seasons are the basic 'metronome' of this planet and have laid down the primary energy rhythm under which organic life has evolved. Therefore, the particular qualities and characteristics of each season are reflected inside us, in the anatomy and physiology of our energy system. In fact they have moulded what we are and how we function. As the seasons progress through their cycle – spring, summer, autumn, winter, spring, and so on – the characteristic energy of that season is also emphasized. The Chinese identify a fifth season – late summer or Indian summer – which is seen as the centre point of the year, giving five seasons in all.

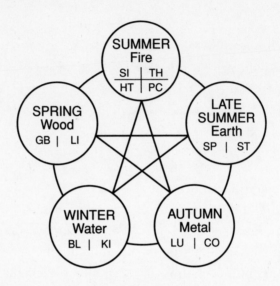

The Five Elements

Each season is related to each Element as follows:

Spring	=	Wood
Summer	=	Fire
Late Summer	=	Earth
Autumn	=	Metal
Winter	=	Water

This is reflected in our internal organs, each one of which is understood to contain the essential energy dynamic of one of the seasons and, therefore, one of the Five Elements. In Oriental medicine there are 12 major organs/functions – heart, small intestine, bladder, kidneys, pericardium, triple heater (a special function that controls temperature), gall bladder, liver, lungs, colon, stomach and spleen.

The Five Elements/Phases interact and operate in very specific and fixed ways and according to definite laws (*see* pp.57–58).

The Eight Diagrams

The Eight Diagrams is the name given to a system devised for understanding and describing change; this directly translates from the Chinese as the *Pa Kua*. The Eight Diagrams are a way of understanding the dynamics of a particular situation and the specific stage or phase in which it is in, between the polarities of Yang and Yin. Knowing this allows us to understand how a particular situation, or configuration of dynamics, may change into another phase or condition. The *Pa Kua* is one of the few ways known to humankind of understanding the basic nature of change and working with it.

The *Pa Kua* describes change as taking place from Yang to Yin in eight stages. Each of these is indicated by what is known as a trigram, a pattern of three lines, any one of which can be yang (unbroken) or yin (broken). These are each given names, which to the Chinese mind indicate their essential nature, as follows:

CH'IEN
Heaven
Creative

CHEN
Thunder
Arousing

K'AN
Water
Abysmal

KEN
Mountain
Keeping Still

K'UN
Earth
Receptive

SUN
Wind
Gentle

LI
Fire
Clinging

TUI
Lake
Joyous

Being able to read a situation in terms of its Eight Diagram dynamics is a way of understanding it and therefore being able to take an appropriate course of action – to align with it, to correct it, to counterbalance it or whatever is needed. This is an old and profound science. It is part of Chinese cosmology and a primary principle of the Chinese view of the basic dynamics of the universe, embodied, as already mentioned, in the great classic the *I Ching*, 'The Book of Changes'. There are many aspects and levels to this science, which have absorbed certain Taoists over their whole lifetime. When the great philosopher Confucius was dying he said that his biggest regret was not spending enough time studying the *I Ching*!

Wu Wei

Wu Wei describes an attitude to the Tao and life. It is a way of looking at the world and what happens, and acting appropriately. It has been translated as 'non-interference', but this has often wrongly been understood as meaning 'doing nothing'. On the contrary, it means correctly understanding something in terms of its energy dynamics and then taking the appropriate action. This has been called 'the Waterway', because the essential nature of water is to fill whatever it comes to and then keep on flowing. Sometimes it is indeed appropriate to not interfere, but at other times it is necessary to put every last ounce of effort and resources into something. You perform the correct action/non-action for the situation. You know what this feels like – it is when something feels 'right' and goes 'perfectly'.

Structure

To understand the energy system, it is necessary to understand what it is and how it works – its anatomy and physiology.

The anatomy of the energy system is its structure, its mechanical reality. This is very different from the way anatomy is understood in the West, where we have limited it to the tangible, what we can see and touch – the cells, tissues, organs and material level of ourselves. In the East this tangible level is considered to be only an expression and manifestation of a more subtle level, a non-tangible energy network, a system of invisible channels/meridians.

To begin to understand and appreciate the energy system, and its importance to our health, we need to first learn some of its essential aspects. This involves such unfamiliar parts of ourselves as the meridian energy channels, the 12 organs/officials, the eight extra meridians, the points, the pulses, the Three Treasures, the Three Tan T'ien, the Three Chou and the basic substances.

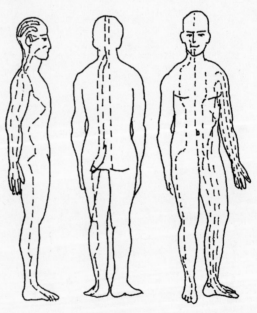

The meridians

Meridian energy channels are lines of energy which run all over the body and connect everything together. There are 12 organ meridians, eight extra meridians, and other connecting and meeting channels, for a total of 35 in all.

Organs/officials are the 12 major internal organs described earlier. Like an official of a country, each of these has a specific function to perform and responsibility to uphold. Each one has its own separate meridian, which is named after it, e.g. the heart meridian, the small intestine meridian, etc. The other organs we are familiar with in Western anatomy – the brain, the uterus, etc. – do not have their own individual meridians but many meridians pass through them. They are known as 'peculiar organs'.

The eight extra meridians are the reservoirs of energy. They are known as 'the oceans of energy', places where energy can be drawn from when needed, or which can hold and accommodate any excess. These are tremendously important channels, for they also act to co-ordinate everything.

The energy points are small centres of *chi* just below the surface of the skin and mostly along meridian pathways. They have come to be called 'acupoints', because they are what is used in acupuncture. They connect with, and affect, the deeper internal energy levels and all of the organs and other tissues. There are over 670 major points, each with its own particular spirit and functions. There are also many other extra, special points.

Chi Kung points are the specific energy/acupoints used in practice. There are 12 major Chi Kung points, areas which are especially powerful and significant for all practices, which will be described throughout the text.

The pulses are felt at the wrist. Instead of just the one heart pulse familiar to Western medicine, there are six pulses on each wrist, 12 in all. Each reflects the energy in one of the 12 organs/officials. Reading a person's pulses is the primary diagnostic technique in the East – every traditional doctor does it to every patient, to learn the state of that person's energy, otherwise they would not know what was really going on. This is a difficult and demanding skill – it is said that to master it takes 10 years of regular practice, comparable to playing the concert piano.

The Three Treasures is the name given to the basic categories of our three 'levels'. These are known as *jing*, *chi* and *shen* – essence, energy and spirit. Sometimes these are run together into the one word *jingchishen* (compare this with the term 'body, mind, spirit' in the West). *Jing*/essence is the biological animal energy and the energy inherited from one's parents. This provides the foundation for *chi*/energy, which is created from breathing and eating, and which, in turn, is the basis of *shen*/spirit, which itself has many levels of distinction in the Oriental tradition. There are numerous ways in which *jing*, *chi* and *shen* interact and relate to each other.

The Three Tan Tien are three major centres of energy, also called the Three Elixir Fields. They are located as follows:

1 The Lower Tan Tien: 2–3 inches (5–7 cm) below the navel

2 The Middle Tan Tien: the centre of the chest

3 The Upper Tan Tien: between the eyebrows

The *jing* has its centre in the Lower Tan Tien, the *chi* in the Middle Tan Tien and the *shen* in the Upper Tan Tien. These centres are so important that many Chi Kung exercises are solely concerned with keeping them strong, integrated and balanced. In familiar Western terms the Three Tan Tien could be respectively seen as the centres of our instinct, intuition and inspiration.

The Three Chou are three sections/spaces of the torso:

1 The Upper Chou: from the neck to the diaphragm

2 The Middle Chou: from the diaphragm to the navel

3 The Lower Chou: from the navel down

Each of these houses particular organs and operates within a specific temperature range. It is essential that they are at the correct temperature in order for the internal organs in that area to function properly.

The basic substances are blood and fluids – derived from eating, drinking and breathing – which lubricate, nourish and warm the organs, tissues, joints and skin. They are the basis for sweat, saliva, tears and other body fluids which are necessary for health.

The above anatomical features constitute the basic structure of the energy system, its material foundation. We now need to look at how it all works.

Function

How the energy works is its physiology, its function. There is not much point in knowing what something is if we don't know how it works or how to use it.

Oriental physiology operates, like everything else, within the Tao. The laws and principles are divided into specific categories, the main ones being, again, Yin and Yang (with its subdivision of the Eight Principles), and the Five Elements (with its subdivision of the Table of Correspondences and Family Relations). Other major principles are known as natural cycles and the factors of disease. There follows a brief description of each of these, with indications of how they relate to our internal functioning, energy and health.

Yin/Yang theory describes the principle of opposites and the relative ratio of proportions of Yin and Yang which exist in every given organ or condition. Of the 12 major organs, six are Yin and six are Yang. The six Yin organs are liver, heart, pericardium, spleen, lungs and kidneys. The six Yang organs are gall bladder, small intestine, triple heater, stomach, colon and bladder.

One of the applications of Yin/Yang theory is known as the Eight Principles. This is a way of describing the state of a person's chi according to four pairs of opposites – Yin/Yang, interior/exterior, deficiency/excess and cold/hot. From this it is possible to discover the specific conditions of somebody's energy and therefore know what to do to bring it back to optimum functioning.

The Five Elements operate in a way that could be understood as the body's internal ecology – the pattern of relationships between an organism and its environment. An Element can be defined as any part which has 'irreducible simplicity', something that cannot be divided into smaller units, like a prime number in mathematics. It is a basic constituent component. If the anatomy of the energy system is its geography, the Five Elements are the weather; in the external environment, weather conditions are caused by the activities of the Elements. Weather is a state of the atmosphere with respect to heat, cold, moistness, dryness and wind. It is the same inside us – these same terms describe the internal conditions and relationships of our various organs and functions; they are the internal reflections of the seasons and the atmosphere.

The Five Elements could be described as 'human ecology'. Just as there are serious external environmental problems when things go out of balance, so there will be serious internal environmental problems – symptoms, illness, pain and disorder on physical, emotional, mental and spiritual levels – if we do not maintain our energy system in the right balance. At this present time it is generally recognized that our planet is out of balance. It is sick. Could it be that the Five Element theory is a key to our current serious environmental problems?

The Five Elements describe not only the relationships and interactions which take place inside ourselves, but also between the inside and the outside, between ourselves and the outer world. These relationships are shown in the Table of Correspondences.

Element	Wood	Fire	Earth	Metal	Water
Season	Spring	Summer	Late Summer	Autumn	Winter
Yang Organ	Gall Bladder	Small Intestine Triple Heater	Stomach	Colon	Bladder
Yin Organ	Liver	Heart Pericardium	Spleen	Lungs	Kidney
Emotion	Anger	Joy	Sympathy	Grief	Fear
Colour	Green	Red	Yellow	White	Blue
Sound	Shouting	Laughing	Singing	Weeping	Groaning
Taste	Sour	Bitter	Sweet	Pungent	Salty
Smell	Rancid	Scorched	Fragrant	Rotten	Putrid
Opening	Eyes	Tongue	Mouth	Nose	Ears
Tissue	Tendons	Blood Vessels	Flesh	Skin and Hair	Bones
Climate	Wind	Heat	Damp	Dry	Cold
Process	Birth	Growth	Transformation	Harvest	Storage
Direction	East	South	Centre	West	North

Table of Correspondences

The Table of Correspondences describes the relationships between the meridians, organs, seasons, emotions, colours, sounds, tissues, etc. It contains profound information on how we work as an integrated whole. The value of understanding these basic correspondences, and integrating them into our way of thinking and living, cannot be over-emphasized; they give powerful and important insights into ourselves and others. The correspondences are the result of millennia of observation by some of the best and brightest minds. I cannot recommend strongly enough the importance taking the time to study and absorb the information on the Table of Correspondences chart; it is one of the primary ways in which this world of ours works.

Family Relations add another dimension. These are inherent laws which reflect the major personal relationships we have with other people in our everyday lives – the Mother–Child Law, the Brother–Sister Law, the Husband–Wife Law and the Grandparent–Grandchild Law. These all take place within the format of the Five Elements, and reflect the various relationships and interactions that the major organs and functions have with each other. If these relationships are out of order it is like having a dysfunctional family inside yourself. Better to have a happy family.

One of the primary principles of energy physiology is the hierarchical progression which states that the energy moves the blood, the blood feeds the cells and tissues, they in turn constitute the organs and functions, and they all work in relationship to each other within one whole. What is particular to Chi Kung, in terms of this physiological progression, is the principle that 'the mind leads the *chi*'. Therefore, the energy can be controlled by the mind.

External Energy and Natural Cycles

External energy refers to environmental energy. Natural cycles are patterns of environmental energy which greatly influence us because they affect the energy system in major ways. Our energy system – including both the meridian system and the aura field (the bio-electric energy field which surrounds each of our bodies), acts like an antenna which connects the external energy environment (ranging from simple sunlight to distant galaxies) into our internal being. This is how we are directly affected by the energy matrix which is the universe of which we are each one small part.

The primary natural cycles are the 24-hour day, the seven-day week, the 28-day moon cycle and the annual cycle of seasons. The rotations and cycles of the Earth, sun and moon – giving us the day, month and year – are the primary conditioning rhythms and factors of life on this planet. These patterns are so deeply rooted in our being that we usually have no separate sense of them, just as we have no separate sense of gravity. They are part of what we are. They are the conditions under which biological life evolved. They are our metronome. We even measure our life by how many rotations around the sun have passed since our birth; it would all be different if we lived on another planet. Because they affect us so pervasively these cycles deserve further description.

The Day

During the 24-hour day the chi moves like a tidal wave through each of the 12 major organ meridians, cresting in each one for a two-hour period, in an exact sequence which is the same for everybody. This is related to, and driven by, the relative position of the Earth to the sun as the Earth rotates on its axis and just where on Earth you are at a given time. This is the reason underlying 'jet lag'.

The Week

Although this is not within the usual Oriental system there is reasonable cause for speculation that there is a relationship between the fact that there are seven days in the week and seven energy centres in our central core channel. There are also seven layers to the aura which surrounds our bodies and it has been said that there are seven layers to the atmosphere around the Earth. In some traditions this is understood to relate to the energetic influence of the seven major planets.

The Month

During the course of the 28-day moon cycle the chi moves up the centre line of the back, reaching a peak at the crown at full moon, and down the centre of the front to the valley at the perineum when the moon is new. The force of this energy cycle controls the tides, women's menstrual cycles and when some people become 'lunatics'.

The Year

During the course of the year, the chi peaks in one of the Five Elements/sets of organs in each of the five seasons. This explains why some people always feel better, or worse, in a particular season or time of year.

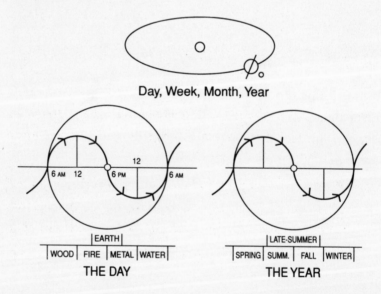

Day, Week, Month, Year

THE DAY

THE YEAR

These interacting cycles are a biological clock which runs like the classic wind-up mechanism of Western physics. It is the same for everybody. If we have a problem, weakness, dysfunction or illness in a particular organ/energy system, or a particular combination of them, then this will show up at the relevant time and we will feel ill, tired, exhausted, unwell, spaced out, etc. Recurrent symptoms may also occur at that time. In order to have some awareness and control over our energy it is as important to understand the effects and consequences of these natural cycles as it is to know how to operate the gears in a car. Stay in only one gear and the journey through life could be slightly problematic and uncomfortable – or even very difficult!

What to Avoid

The factors of disease are influences which adversely affect the energy and push it into disharmony. The two major sub-divisions of this are external and internal causes.

- *External factors include*: Adverse environmental conditions of wind, heat, humidity, dryness and cold; trauma and accident; poor, spoiled or detrimental food, drink and nutrition; pathogenic organisms; pollution, toxins and poisoning.

- *Internal factors include:* Deficient or excess emotions of anger, joy, sympathy, grief or fear; inappropriate emotional attitudes or beliefs; detrimental emotional relationships, situations and environments; maladies of the spirit.

Being aware of these factors allows us to avoid, or diminish, their influence as much as possible.

Summary

The anatomy and physiology of the energy system are the basis of health and well-being. Having one's energy system functioning improperly can cause the energy to become blocked, stagnant, deficient, excessive, polluted, too hot or too cold, and can result in all manner of illness and dysfunction. So, if a person keeps their energy strong and clear they will be at their best – and Chi Kung is one of the ways to do this. There's every possible reason to practise!

Chapter Four

Chi Kung Practices for Common Conditions

- Introduction
- Relaxation Chi Kung
- Head and Face Chi Kung
- Eye Chi Kung
- Nose and Teeth Chi Kung
- Ear Chi Kung
- Neck Chi Kung
- Shoulder and Arm Chi Kung
- Chest Chi Kung
- Abdomen Chi Kung
- Waist Chi Kung
- Legs and Feet Chi Kung
- Summary

气 功

Chapter Four

Chi Kung Practices for Common Conditions

Introduction

Chi Kung healing has many different styles and applications. Three main categories are:

  * external exercise sequences or postures, known as 'Dynamic Chi Kung' or 'Wei Dan'
  * internal meditation practices, known as 'Static Chi Kung' or 'Nei Dan'
  * the transmission of chi from a practitioner to a patient for healing, known as 'External Chi Healing' or 'Bu Qi'

Chi Kung healing practices in many ways follow the same diagnostic and treatment procedures as acupuncture or any of the other forms of Oriental medicine. Indeed, in the broadest sense Chi Kung can be considered the foundation of all of the

Oriental healing forms, because they are all ways of working with energy.

Chi Kung treatment requires the practitioner to develop refined awareness and control of their own energy, and also an advanced degree of sensitivity in feeling another person's energy and knowing how to treat it. It is 'needleless acupuncture'. It is an extension of the same skills and abilities. In some ways Chi Kung is a post-graduate level of Oriental practice. Knowing your own energy and how to control it has often been a prerequisite for medical training in China.

Chi Kung healers can perform a whole compendium of treatment on a patient, for all kinds of conditions. Experienced practitioners are currently rare in the West and are mostly Asians who have trained in the East. However, practitioners are now becoming increasingly available as Chi Kung is beginning to be integrated into the curricula of the Oriental medicine schools in the West, as it has been in China for centuries, and Westerners are going to the East to train and develop their skills.

Chi Kung exercises can be used for self-treating a range of conditions. There is an increasing repertory of such specific practices for particular conditions appearing in textbooks and technical manuals. Some of these are complex and require a knowledge of foundational practices or personal instruction from a teacher, but the following is a set of Dynamic Chi Kung practices that anybody can do. They will not only help maintain good health, but are also applicable for a wide range of common conditions: headaches, dizziness, the common cold, ear and eye problems, toothache, hayfever, stiff neck, joint pain, aching limbs, coughing, indigestion, colon problems, lower back pain, sciatica, lumbago and more. Such a list is possible because these Chi Kung exercises are focused on the meridian system of the body. So they relate not only to all of the internal organs, but also the associated tissues, muscles, regional geography, sense organs and other functions. Each area of the body is covered in the following order:

Relaxation

Head and Face

Eyes

Nose and Teeth

Ears

Neck

Shoulders and Arms

Chest

Abdomen

Waist

Legs and Feet

To begin with, they should be learned in the order here, then later, when you have the feel and sense of them, try the variations described in the summary of this chapter (*see* p.98).

Relaxation Chi Kung

Purpose: Exercises to generate a state of internal relaxation and prepare you for further practice.

This can be performed standing, sitting or lying. If you are standing, let your arms just hang naturally down by your sides. If you are sitting, let your hands rest on your thighs, palms facing upwards. If you are lying, let your arms lie by your sides, palms up.

- Calm your breathing. Clear your mind. Half close or fully close the eyes. Concentrate on the Lower Tan Tien, 2–3 inches (5–7 cm) below your navel. Place the tip of the tongue on the roof of your mouth, behind your teeth, to connect the central Governor and Conception meridians.

- As you breathe in, bring your attention and energy to the sides of your head, and as you slowly breathe out send your mind and energy down through your neck and shoulders to your upper arms, elbows, forearms, wrists, hands and fingers, relaxing and releasing any tension as you go.

- As you breathe in, bring your attention and energy to your face, and as you slowly breathe out, send your mind and energy down the *front* of your body, through your neck, chest, abdomen, upper legs, knees, lower legs, feet and toes, relaxing and releasing any tension as you go.

• As you breathe in, bring your attention and energy to the back of your head, and as you slowly breathe out, send your mind and energy down the *back* of your body, over the rear of your head and down your neck, back, waist, upper legs, back of the knees, lower legs and ankles to the soles of your feet, relaxing and releasing any tension as you go.

• As you breathe in, bring your attention and energy to your head, and as you slowly breathe out, send your mind and energy down your *whole body* all at the same time, down to your fingers and down your front and back to your feet. Deeply relax your whole being.

Repeat this whole sequence 3, 5, 7, 9 times or more.

Head and Face Chi Kung

Purpose: These exercises activate the meridians of your head and face. They can be used to prevent and treat conditions such as headache, dizziness, tension, tiredness and the common cold.

Sitting or standing. Relax the body. Clear your mind. Close your eyes. Connect your tongue against the roof of your mouth behind your teeth on the hard palate.

Do all of the following exercises with moderate pressure.

- Bring your hands up to your eyebrows and, using the pads of the three middle fingers of both hands push, upwards from the midpoint of the eyebrows to the hairline 12 times.
- Then, from the middle of the brow, push to the sides, level with the ears, 12 times. Perform this motion as you breathe out.
- Next, using the pads of the fingers, rub the temples in a circular motion, from the front to the top to the back and so on, 12 times.
- Using the palms of your hands, rub from the sides of the forehead down either side of the face to the chin, then back up again 12 times. Imagine you are washing your face with the energy in your palms.
- Use all five fingers of each hand to comb your hair and massage your scalp from the front to back of your head 12 times.

- Place the fingertips in front of the ears and then sweep up and then over and behind your ears and on down the back of the neck to your shoulders six times. Keep your shoulders relaxed.
- Interlock the fingers and place the hands on top of your head, then slowly rub from the top of the head to the base of the neck six times.

These exercises energize and stimulate all of the six Yang meridians of the head – small intestine, bladder, triple heater, gall bladder, colon and stomach – and also the main Governor meridian. They are excellent for the complexion and are one of the best forms of beauty care. They are beneficial for all functions of the head and face. They freshen you up and make you feel awake.

Eye Chi Kung

Purpose: These practices can be used to benefit the eyes and eyesight by stimulating the surrounding energy channels. They can help to relieve painful, swollen eyes, tiredness and congestion.

Sitting, standing or lying, relax. Look straight ahead or close your eyes.

This practice involves moving the eyes in a figure of eight pattern. Imagine the *chi* moving in the socket and let the eyeballs move along with it.

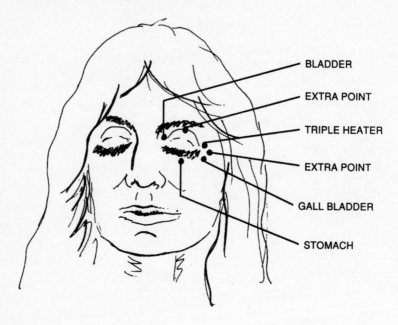

- Begin by moving the left eye in the upper inner corner at the point Bladder 1/Eyes Bright, then move slowly along the top of the left socket out to the edge, then back inwards again along the bottom edge of the socket. Next, transfer to the right eye at the right Bladder 1 point, move it along the upper edge of the right socket out to the right side, then return along the lower border of the socket back to the centre. Repeat this eight times.

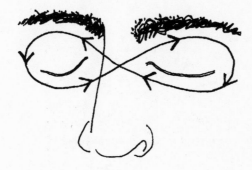

Points around the eyes

- Press the tips of your thumbs against the Bladder 1 point, using moderate pressure, and focus your mind there. When inhaling, press against the point. When exhaling, press gently against the eyeballs themselves. Do this eight times.
- Close your eyes. Rub the pads of the thumbs together to make them warm, then gently rub them across the corresponding eyelid, from the inside of each eye to the edges, 12 times.

• With the pads of your three middle fingers, rub in a circular motion around the outer rim of your eye sockets 12 times.

These practices stimulate and activate six major acupoints around the eyes, which are the beginning or ending points of meridian lines, or are special eye points.

Nose and Teeth Chi Kung

Purpose: These exercises can be used to help prevent and treat diseases of the nose, mouth and teeth. They are useful for such conditions as the common cold, runny nose, hayfever, inflammation of the mucous membranes and toothache.

Sitting or standing, breathe evenly and relax.

• Use the backs of the middle joint of your thumbs. Rub them together until they are warm, then rub them either side of the nose, in the cleft by the sides of the nostrils, up to the bridge and back down again. The major point here is Colon 20 (Welcome Fragrance), either side of your nostrils. Rub five times or more.

• With the tip of either one of the middle fingers, press the mid-brow point, between the eyes at the top of the nose at the bridge, and rotate around it with your fingertip in a circular motion – rotating to the left when inhaling five times, and rightward when exhaling five times.

• Knock the upper and lower teeth together 36 times and swallow the saliva.

• Grit your teeth together then slowly relax 12 times. Breathe naturally and focus your mind on your teeth.

These exercises stimulate the major meridians affecting the nose, mouth and teeth, and help with any related conditions or symptoms in this area. They also encourage deeper and better breathing.

Ear Chi Kung

Purpose: These exercises clear the meridian channels and open the ears. They help with all ear conditions, such as deteriorating hearing, tinnitus/ringing in the ears, Menière's disease and earache.

Sitting or standing, close your eyes and relax. Clear your mind. Breathe naturally. Listen inwardly with your ears.

- Press your palms against your ears so that the point in the centre of your palms is directly opposite the ear opening, your fingers lying along the back of your head.

- With your hands in the same position, let your index fingers slip off the top of your middle fingers and gently 'flick' the base of your head and skull. Do this 24 times. Listen to the drumming sound. This practice is appropriately called 'Beat the Heavenly Drum'.

- Press your palms against your earholes, increasing the internal pressure, then release them. Do this rapidly but gently. Vary the frequency and pressure. Repeat 10 times.

- Gently squeeze and pinch your ears until they feel warm. Starting from the front, squeeze along the auricle/rim of the ear up the front then down the rear to the ear lobe. Squeeze and pinch your ear lobes.

- With your thumbs and the side and tip of your index fingers, rub, stretch and massage the inside and back of your ear flaps until they feel warm.

These simple exercises will greatly benefit your ears by stimulating the energy and therefore the blood circulation. It has recently been discovered that there are nerve endings in the ear flaps which connect with the whole body – an example of our integrated, holistic nature. There is now a sub-speciality in the field of acupuncture known as 'ear acupuncture'. Some of the ear points have been found to be indispensible in acupuncture's remarkably effective detox programmes for drugs, alcohol and smoking.

Ear Chi Kung has many benefits throughout the body and can be easily integrated into normal life. It is so beneficial you would do well to make a good habit of it.

Neck Chi Kung

Purpose: These exercises can be used to relieve a stiff and aching neck, shoulder and arm pain, and other associated conditions. They activate the energy channels, relax the muscles and tendons, and help with the joints.

Sitting or standing, relax the neck, breathe naturally and look straight ahead.

- Press the pads of the thumbs against the energy points Gall Bladder 20 (Wind Pond), which are located at the base of your skull in the biggest 'valley' between the major two sets of muscles. Your fingertips rest on the back of your head. In small circular motions rub lightly five times. Lightly tap and knock these points with the joined tips of the thumb and the three middle fingers 30 times.

- Tip the head slightly forward and downwards, then, while exhaling, use the pads of the fingers and push from the base of the head, where it joins the top of the neck, down either side to the base of the neck, then out to the tips of the shoulders five times. Do both sides together or do one side first and then the other – left first for males and right first for females.
- When inhaling, slowly turn the head and neck leftwards from front to back, and then, when exhaling, from back to front. Then reverse the direction of the pattern to the right side. Repeat nine times.
- Interlace your fingers behind your neck and, while inhaling, press forward with your fingers and press back with your head so that your face and eyes look upwards. Repeat nine times.

These exercises activate the main meridian of the Governor channel and also the bladder, gall bladder and triple heater meridians. They affect many energy points in this area, which in turn stimulate the muscles, tendons, bones and other tissues. This is an important practice to help prevent such conditions as arthritis from developing in the neck.

Shoulder and Arm Chi Kung

Purpose: These exercises can be used to prevent and treat diseases of the upper extremities. They are helpful with such conditions as arm pains, numbness and weakness, swelling and poor circulation, and is good for the joints.

———————

Sitting or standing, clear your mind. Relax your body. Breathe easily.

- Using a lightly clenched fist or cupped hand, gently pound the muscles along the top of the opposite shoulder, then slowly work down the back of one arm to the wrist. Repeat this three to five times. This works down the three Yang meridians of the arms – small intestine, triple heater and colon.
- Turn the arm over, so that it is facing upwards, and again gently pound down from the top to the bottom. Repeat this three to five times. This works down the three Yin meridians of the arm – heart, pericardium and lungs.
- Do the same to the other arm.
- In a sitting position, place the right hand on the right thigh, palm facing upwards. Push and rub with the left hand down the inner side of the right arm, from the inside shoulder to the hand. Exhale slowly as you do this. Then, as you inhale, turn the arm and hand over and push and rub upwards from the back of the hand up to the outside shoulder. Do this three times.
- Do the same to the other arm.
- Bend the right arm in front of you, and with your left thumb, press and knead the energy point at the elbow. This point is

located on the upper side of the elbow halfway between the outside edge of the crease of the elbow and the mound of the bone. Do this 36 times. Then do this at the left elbow, using the right thumb. This is a major point with good benefits.

• Now place your hand out in front of you, with palm facing down and with thumb and forefinger spread apart. Press, knead and rotate the point between your thumb and forefinger, at the top of the valley where the bones meet, using the thumb of the opposite hand. This is another major energy point. Do this 36 times. Reverse sides.

As mentioned, these practices activate the three Yin meridians and the three Yang meridians which run down and up the arms. They are also very good for the shoulders.

Chest Chi Kung

Purpose: These exercises sequences are good for many conditions of the chest – the basic respiratory and cardiac functions. They can be used to prevent, relieve and treat stuffiness of the chest, coughing, excess sputum, difficult breathing, shortness of breath, chest pain and more.

Sitting or standing, breathe evenly and relax.

- Starting from the notch at the base of the front of your throat, while exhaling use the flat of the fingers to rub down the centre line of the breastbone, the sternum, down to its base, 36 times.

- With the pads of the fingers, rub the point of the Middle Tan Tien – Conception 17 (Within the Breast) – in a small circular motion 36 times. Concentrate your attention at this point. Feel the area get warm. This point feeds into the whole chest area.

- Starting from the top of the mid-line of your chest, when exhaling push with the right palm from the centre line of the chest to the left side 5–10 times. Continue on down to the bottom of your chest bone. Pause when inhaling. Then, using the left palm, repeat the procedure again from top to bottom, pushing from the centre to the right side 5–10 times. Pay attention with your mind.

- With the flat of both palms and with fingers pointed towards each other, tips 2 inches (5 cm) apart, rub down from just below the ribs either side of the centre line to the level of the waist. Do this while exhaling. This sends down any 'rebellious' energy which may be rising up into the chest and causing problems. Do this 5–10 times.

- When you exhale, rub with the flat of the palms from under the armpits down to the waist level. Do this 5–10 times.

These practices activate, open and clear the energy channels of the chest and help with all related problems in this area.

Abdomen Chi Kung

Purpose: This set of practices can be used to prevent and treat diseases and syndromes of the abdomen. It also has the function of strengthening the spleen and stomach, regulating the Middle Chou, tonifying the kidneys and generally building energy. Conditions such as gastritis, ulcers, digestive problems and colitis can be helped with this practice.

Do these in a lying position. Relax your body. Touch the tip of your tongue against the palate. Breathe normally.

- Place the palm of your right hand on the centre of your solar plexus – Conception 12 (Middle Duct). This point regulates the stomach and spleen. Rub and rotate from right to left in small circles 36 times.
- Place the centre of the palm of the right hand over the navel and rub and rotate from right to left in small circles 36 times.
- Place the left hand on the centre line of the lower abdomen at the Lower Tan Tien point (the Elixir Field), with the right hand on top of it. Rub and rotate from right to left in small circles 36 times.
- When exhaling, using the tips of the four fingers of the two hands, or the whole palms, push down the mid-line

of the abdomen from the bottom of the chest bone down to the top of the pubic bone. Do this 12 times.

* Pinch, lift, release and lightly percuss the whole area of the lower abdomen with the five fingers, 25 or more times.

This set of practices activates the meridians of the lower abdomen and also stimulates some of the major points in this area. It especially helps with many aspects of digestion.

Waist Chi Kung

Purpose: This set is good for preventing and treating diseases and discomfort in the lower back, soreness of the waist and disc problems. They strengthen the bones and muscles, reinforce the waist and tonify the kidneys.

Standing with the legs apart, relax and breathe easily.

* With hands on your waist, elbows out to your sides, rotate the hips to the left 36 times. Repeat this to the right 36 times.
* Clench both hands and gently pound and drum the area of the lower back, starting from the bottom of the ribs and

moving   down   to   the   back   of   the   pelvis,
12 times.

* Using your palms and fingers, rub down your back, from
  the bottom of the ribs down to the base of the pelvis,
  until this area gets warm. You can rub straight down or
  slowly work your way down in small circular motions.

There are many acupuncture points in this area which feed into
the lower abdominal organs and which also support the lower back
muscles that are often overused. These simple procedures soothe,
relax and heal this important region. People commonly rub their
lower back, but these practices add the awareness of your energy
system. You get much greater benefit for a very slight adjustment.

Legs and Feet Chi Kung

Purpose: These practices operate by stimulating the three Yang
meridians – bladder, gall bladder and stomach – and the three
Yin meridians – kidneys, liver and spleen. They can be used to
help treat such conditions as sciatica, arthritis, lumbago and
numbness of the legs. They can also help prevent the stagnation
and pooling of blood which can lead to varicose veins. (Please
note: If you already have varicose veins, do not do this exercise.
Massaging varicose veins is contraindicated.)

Sitting, calm and clear your mind and relax.

- Gently stretch one leg forward. With the cupped palms of the hands, gently pat down the outside of the leg, from the top down to the bottom, then down to the foot, three to five times. Follow this with your mind and concentration. Then do the same movement down the inside of the same leg, three to five times.

- Repeat this on the opposite leg.

- Again on the first leg, gently push and rub the outside, from the top down to the foot, kneading the muscles. Then move up the inside of the leg, again gently kneading and rubbing and following the movement with your mind. Do this three to five times.

These procedures stimulate and activate the energy channels of your legs and help promote the circulation of energy and blood.

Summary

The foregoing series of exercises can help prevent and treat a wide variety of conditions. They can be practised in various ways:

- They can be performed in one complete sequence, thereby getting a full workout and energy stimulation of the major meridians.

- One practice can be done each day, so that over the course of one and a half weeks a total energy-body sequence is completed.

- One or more practices can be done if a person has a problem in a particular area, or a certain place is affected by work – for example, drivers or massage therapists may emphasize neck, shoulder and arm Chi Kung; salespeople may emphasize leg Chi Kung; students or people who read and write for a living may emphasize eye Chi Kung.

- Any of these practices can be done on an 'as needed' basis. If a person has just been bending over working in the garden all afternoon, has walked up and down a mountain or spent the day using their brain, then they should use the appropriate Chi Kung. The practices are tools to be used as and when needed.

- It is best to do these practices often and incorporate them into a daily routine; however, doing them just once a week is far better than not doing them at all.

If a person begins by practising conscientiously, so that they develop the feel, knack and skill of the practices, then they will find that they begin to do them automatically and naturally. It is important to begin slowly, as it takes time to get the feel and flow of it all, and then gradually integrate the exercises into daily routine.

These practices are a little more complicated than rubbing and massaging yourself, which everybody does instinctively. However, because they are focused on the meridian energy system they have a much deeper and more profound effect than unconscious self-massage. They act to treat and stimulate the meridian energy system, and therefore all of the internal organs and functions. This is self-massage with the additional purpose and intent of working with the energy system. At its best it not only makes a person feel good, but also has the additional tremendous advantage of being preventative medicine. Just because it seems easy, do not underestimate its benefits.

Chi Kung is simple. It's effective. It's free. And it can belong to anybody, for life — if they just take the time to learn these few simple exercises.

Chapter Five

Favourite Classics

- Introduction
- Cleansing your Energy
- Smile – at Yourself
- Standing like a Stake
- The Microcosmic Orbit
- The Macrocosmic Orbit
- Summary

气 功

Chapter Five

Favourite Classics

Introduction

Over long accumulated history certain Chi Kung practices have emerged which have stayed the course and become established as well loved and treasured 'classics'.

There are many of these classics. Some are simple and straightforward and anybody can do them with a little instruction; some can be done at either introductory or advanced levels; others are so complex that they require personal instruction over an extended period of time, and then grow in subtlety and sensitivity to the point where, like classical ballet, they enter into the realm of refined art. Such complex, refined practices are, for example, the Five Animal Frolics (Wu Qin Xi), the Eight Pieces of Brocade (Ba Duan Jin), the Muscle and

Tendon-Changing Classic (Yi Jin Jing), Shadow Boxing (Tai Chi Chuan) and Wild Goose Chi Kung (Dayan Chi Kung). All of these now have many, many variations which have evolved over the course of history, as various people, families or schools have each slowly developed their own individual style, form or tradition. They are all complex and difficult to describe adequately in the context of a book such as this. Whole books are devoted to just one form or style (*see* Bibliography). These practices are best learned slowly and carefully from an experienced practitioner and teacher. The following, however, are some adapted classics in simplified form, which can be usefully and effectively learned and practised.

But before beginning practice, some suggestions. Take your time. Work with yourself carefully. Build up gradually and find your own comfortable and right level. You are the only judge of how much is enough and how much is too much. The best guide is how you respond and feel, and nobody else can know this except yourself. Your response is determined by such factors as the state of your energy, your age, your physical condition, the time of day and of the year and the location that you are in. If you take time, apply patience and proceed slowly, you will gradually begin to develop the 'sense' and the 'feel' of your energy. So practise with your best attention!

Cleansing your Energy

Doing this exercise helps to clear any negative energy – which can come from many different sources – out of your energy system. It helps purify and cleanse you.

- *Standing or sitting, feet shoulder width apart, arms hanging relaxed down by your sides, eyes closed, clear your mind and relax.*

- As you breathe in, slowly raise your arms up, out to the sides, palms facing upwards, until they are over your head, shoulder width apart. Turn the palms over so that they are facing towards the sky, slightly bent at the elbows. Breathe out.

- As you breathe in, again use your mind to draw the energy of the sun, moon and heavens into your palms, soaking it up as if they were sponges so that they become full with fresh, clean energy. Breathe in a number of times until you feel that your palms are 'loaded' with energy.

- As you breathe out, use this fresh energy in your palms to clean out any negative energy that may have accumulated inside you. Turn your palms over so that they face down towards you. Then bring your hands slowly down either side of you and, using your mind, radiate the fresh energy from your palms down the whole length of your body so that you clean out any negative energy. Beginning at the top of your head, continue down through your body and legs to the bottom of your feet and out through the soles of your feet into the ground. Send this 3 feet (1 metre) beneath you, outside your personal energy field.

• Repeat 3, 6, 9, 15 or more times.

Check how you feel after doing this exercise. Do it any time you just want to freshen up.

Smile – at Yourself

In the following practice you are going to smile at yourself, *inside* – at your heart, lungs, liver, kidneys and spleen – and then gather your energy at your navel. Each organ is accompanied by a list of its corresponding characteristics – the colour, temperature, season, emotions, sound and coupled Yang organ. (The Yang organ is automatically affected by the practice.) Using your mind, activate these correspondences when you smile at each organ.

Standing, sitting or lying in a comfortable and relaxed position, close your eyes and clear your mind.

- Activate a memory, thought, image or picture which causes you to smile – one of those soft, warm, gentle, friendly smiles.
- Gather the positive energy of this smile at your forehead, at the point between your eyes, Yin Tang (the Original Cavity of the Spirit). Let this accumulate and grow there, like warm water slowly filling a deep bowl.
- Touch your tongue to the roof of your mouth, on the hard palate just behind your teeth, and find the point which tingles most or feels 'right'.

Smile at your Heart

As you breathe in, draw this warm energy down from your brow through your tongue and throat to your heart.

The colour of your heart is	Red.
The temperature is	Hot.
The season is	Summer.
The emotions are	Joy and Anxiety.
The sound is	Laughing.
The coupled organs are	Small Intestines, Pericardium and Triple Heater.

As you slowly breathe in and out, hold your smiling energy in your heart and send it your love. Let your heart fill with your energy. Hold your mind there.

Breathe in and out 3, 6, 9 or more times.

Smile at your Lungs

As you breathe in, draw this warm smiling energy from your heart to your lungs.

The colour is of your lungs is	White.
The temperature is	Cool.
The season is	Autumn.
The emotions are	Grief and Purification.
The sound is	Weeping.
The coupled organ is the	Colon.

As you slowly breathe in and out, hold your smiling energy in your lungs and send them your love. Let your lungs fill with your energy. Hold your mind there.

Breathe in and out 3, 6, 9 or more times.

Smile at your Liver

As you breathe in, draw this warm smiling energy from your lungs to your liver, which is located under the rib cage on the right side.

The colour is of your liver is Green.

The temperature is Warm.

The season is Spring.

The emotions are Anger and Power.

The sound is Shouting.

The coupled organ is the Gall Bladder.

As you slowly breathe in and out, hold your smiling energy in your liver and send it your love. Let your liver fill with your energy. Hold your mind there.

Breathe in and out 3, 6, 9 or more times.

Smile at your Kidneys

As you breathe in, draw this warm smiling energy from your liver to your kidneys.

Your kidneys are about the size of clenched fists, halfway between the bottom of your back rib cage and the top of your pelvis, either side of the spine and about one third inside your body from your back.

The colour of your kidneys is Blue/Black.

The temperature is Cold.

The season is Winter.

The emotions are Fear and Awe.

The sound is   Groaning.
The coupled organ is the Bladder.

As you slowly breathe in and out, hold your smiling energy in your kidneys and send them your love. Let your kidneys fill with your energy. Hold your mind there.

Breathe in and out 3, 6, 9 or more times.

Smile at your Spleen

As you breathe in, draw this warm smiling energy from your kidneys to your spleen.

Your spleen is located under your rib cage on the left side, on the opposite side to your liver.

The colour of your spleen is Yellow.
The temperature is   Mild.
The season is   LateSummer/Indian
                              Summer.
The emotions are   Sympathy and Worry.
The sound is   Singing.
The coupled organ is the   Stomach.

As you slowly breathe in and out, hold your smiling energy in your spleen (and its associated organ the pancreas) and send them your love. Let your spleen and pancreas fill with your energy. Hold your mind there.

Breathe in and out 3, 6, 9 or more times.

Gathering at your Navel

Finally, bring your energy from your spleen to your navel and hold it there. Let go of your smile and disconnect your tongue from the roof of your mouth. Slowly 'wind' your energy in to your navel, through your heart, lungs, liver, kidneys and spleen, clearing each organ as you go, until your energy is finally all gathered in your navel.

Place the centre of your palm over the navel – left hand first for men, right hand first for women – then cover the back of that hand with the palm of the other hand. Concentrate your attention, mind and will-power at your navel and seal the energy in there.

Pay attention to how you feel. Find a word, phrase, image or symbol that describes how you now feel and remember it. (Better still, write it down after you have finished.)

Slowly open your eyes and return your attention to the outside world.

You have just completed an internal practice of the primary classical Chinese system of the Five Elements, which calms, relaxes and heals all of the major internal organ systems.

Standing like a Stake

This practice brings external energy into you. It is a way to increase your total energy volume. Use it when you are feeling tired or want to just get a little more chi when you need it.

_____

Standing, feet shoulder width apart and flat on the ground, arms hanging loosely by your sides, knees loose and slightly bent, close, or half-close, your eyes. Regulate your breathing so that it is smooth, slow and even. Put your attention inside yourself.

- Bending your arms at the elbows, raise your lower arms until they are at a right angle to your body, with your hands and palms facing downwards towards the ground, elbows soft and relaxed.

- Using your mind, as you breathe in, gather the energy of the Earth at the soles of your feet and also at the centre of your palms.

- Next, as you breathe in, gather the energy of Heaven at the point on the crown, the very top of your head.

- Now, as you breathe in, draw the energy of Earth up your legs to your perineum, then up the centre line of your abdomen to your navel. Next, draw the energy in your palms up your arms and shoulders to meet at the centre of your chest, then draw it down to your navel.

- Following this, draw the Heaven energy at your crown down the front of your head and over your nose. Connect your tongue to the roof of your mouth and send your energy down to your navel.

- Feel the energy from Heaven and Earth enter you and fill you.

- Let your breathing grow deeper, longer and more relaxed and send your attention and energy to your navel. Pay attention to how your body feels. Find a word, phrase, image or symbol which describes this feeling and remember it.

- Do this practice for one minute to begin with. After this feels comfortable, extend it to five minutes, then later to 10 minutes, 30 minutes, or even an hour or more.

There are many variations of this practice, which is known as Zhan Zhuang. These are excellently described in the book *The Way of Energy* by Master Lam Kam Chuen (*see* Bibliography). They are a way to build up internal strength and power without vigorous or strenuous exercise, and are therefore perfect practices for older people.

The Microcosmic Orbit

The Microcosmic Orbit is one of the most important basic practices in Chi Kung, because it has such a pervasive effect on so many levels. It is also known as 'the Lesser Heavenly Cycle' (Xiao Jiu Tien). It connects, and opens up, all of the major organ meridians. All of these meridians have 'meeting' points along the Governor meridian or the Conception meridian and doing the Microcosmic Orbit activates these points. It is the primary circuit which every other channel connects with.

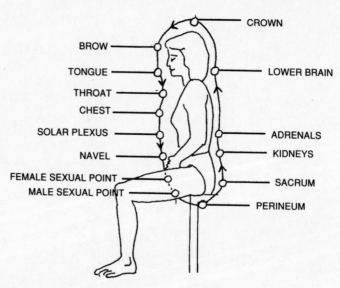

CROWN

BROW

TONGUE — LOWER BRAIN

THROAT

CHEST

SOLAR PLEXUS — ADRENALS

NAVEL — KIDNEYS

FEMALE SEXUAL POINT — SACRUM

MALE SEXUAL POINT

PERINEUM

The Microcosmic Orbit

Sit on the edge of a chair (unless you have back problems, in which case sit whichever way is most comfortable but keeping your spine in an upright posture). Don't slump or lounge, as it blocks the energy. Place your knees shoulder width apart and your feet flat on the ground facing forward. Close your eyes. Put your attention inside yourself.

Clasp your palms in front of you – left facing up and right facing down on top of left. If it is comfortable, let your palms rest in your lap. If this is not comfortable, let your forearms rest gently and lightly against the sides of your abdomen.

The Navel

Put your attention into your navel. Imagine that you are breathing in and out through your navel, until you begin to feel an energy sensation there – this may feel warm, or full, or tingling. See your navel as a clockface, with 12 o'clock at the top, 3 on the left side, 6 at the bottom and 9 at the right side. You are going to spiral out from the navel. To 'open' the navel, start at 12 o'clock and begin by moving the spiral to the right/counter-clockwise for men, and to the left/clockwise for women. Now, using your mind, continue spiralling out nine complete revolutions, in ever-increasing spirals. The bottom of the ninth, final spiral should touch the top of the pubic bone on the centre line of your lower abdomen and the top of the spiral should touch the base of the sternum on the centre line of your upper abdomen.

When you have completed this procedure, reverse direction and spiral back inwards, to the navel, in the course of six revolutions, until you return to the centre of the navel. Move in the opposite direction to the one you began in – to the left/clockwise for men and to the right/counter-clockwise for women. Check how this now feels. Remember this sensation.

This procedure has opened up your energy at the navel and turned it on.

The Sexual Point

As you breathe out, use your mind to send your energy down the front mid-line of your abdomen to your sexual point. For women the sexual point is 2–3 inches (5–7 cm) below the navel. For men it is at the top of the pubic bone. Hold your energy there with your mind. Breathe in and out at this point three or more times. Notice how this feels.

The Perineum

As you breathe out, use your mind to send your energy to your perineum – the area of soft tissue between the top of your legs and between your genitals and anus. Hold your energy there. Breathe in and out at your perineum three or more times. Notice how this feels.

The Base of the Pelvis

Next, use your mind to direct your attention and energy to the base of your pelvis, to the point where the pelvis meets your tail-bone, the coccyx. Hold your attention there. Breathe in and out at this point three or more times. Notice how this feels.

Opposite the Navel

Now, send your attention and energy to the point in the centre of your back opposite your navel. Hold your mind, attention and energy at this point. Breathe in and out here three or more times. Notice how this feels.

The Adrenals

Send your mind and energy up the middle of your back to the point opposite the centre of your solar plexus. This is the adrenal point. Hold your mind there. Breathe in and out at this point three or more times. Notice how this feels.

Base of the Skull

Now, send your energy up the mid-line of your back to the point at the base of your skull. Hold your attention there. Breathe in and out at this point for three or more breaths. Notice how this feels.

Crown of the Head

Next, bring your energy to the crown point, on the very top of your head. Feel your energy accumulate there. Breathe in and out three or more times. Notice how this feels.

The Brow

Then, bring your energy down the mid-line of the front of your forehead to the point between your eyes. Feel your energy grow warm and soft. Hold your mind there. Breathe in and out three or more times. Notice how this feels.

Roof of your Mouth

Now, connect the tip of your tongue to the roof of your mouth, so that your tongue-tip finds the most sensitive and active spot on the hard palate behind your teeth. You may feel a tingling sensation. Hold your energy there for three or more breaths. Notice how this feels.

The Throat

Bring your attention down through your tongue and throat to the point just below your Adam's apple. Hold your attention, mind and energy there for three or more breaths. Notice how this feels.

Centre of the Chest

Now, bring your mind down the front mid-line of your sternum to the chest point. Hold your mind and energy there. Breathe in and out at this point three or more times. Notice how this feels.

Solar Plexus

Next, bring your energy down to the mid-point of your solar plexus, between the bottom of your sternum and your navel. Hold it there. Breathe in and out at this point three or more times. Notice how this feels.

And Back to the Navel

Finally, bring your energy back home to your navel. Hold your mind and energy there. Pay attention to how this feels. Breathe in and out three or more times.

Does this feel warm or tingling? Does it have a colour? What does it feel like? How do you feel in general? Remember these sensations and feelings, and store them in your energy memory library.

To Continue

If you wish to continue practising at this stage, then you can circulate around the Microcosmic Orbit as long as you feel comfortable with this practice – 3, 6, 9 times or more. But be careful not to overdo this in the early stages of practice.

Sealing your Energy

When you want to end, to seal your energy back into your navel, spiral out with your mind from the middle of your navel nine times, until the outermost spiral touches the top of your pubic bone and the base of your sternum. But, this time, in order to close it down and seal it in, reverse your original direction so that men spiral out to the left/clockwise and women spiral out to the right/counter-clockwise. When you have reached the limit of your sternum and pubic bone, then reverse direction to come back into the centre of your navel in six spirals. Check how you now feel and record it in your memory.

Bathing your Eyes

When you have finished the Microcosmic Orbit, rub your palms together and place them over your eyes. Feel the warmth of your palms calm and refresh your eyes. Then, wash your whole face with the energy in your palms. Finally bring your hands down to just rest any way comfortably on your thighs.

Always end by bringing your energy back into your navel and sealing it there.

Slowly open your eyes and let the outer world come into you. See how you feel now.

————————

You have just completed the Microcosmic Orbit – circulating your energy from your navel down the Yin Conception meridian to your perineum, then up the Yang Governor meridian (up the centre of your back and over your head to your mouth), and then on down the Yin Conception meridian (from your mouth down the front line in the middle of your abdomen) back to your navel.

This practice can be done at different intensities. It is advisable to start lightly and gently at first and slowly increase duration and intensity as you develop. Repeat this exercise whenever you wish, for differing amounts of time or differing numbers of breaths at each point, as you feel the need.

If during the course of this practice you meet an unexpected congestion or energy blockage at some point, then go back through each of the points in the reverse direction, bringing it back to the navel, and seal your energy there. Try the complete practice again at another time. Persevere.

To really get the feel for the Microcosmic Orbit, it is best to get personal instruction from a teacher.

The Macrocosmic Orbit

This practice is based upon the Microcosmic Orbit and reinforces it.

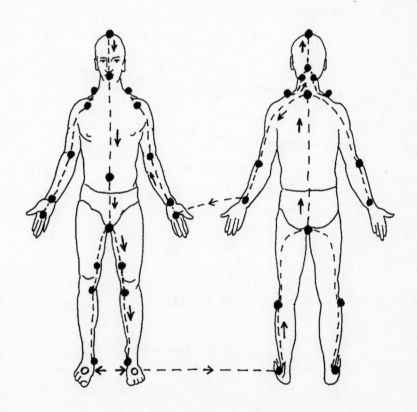

The Macrocosmic Orbit

Stand with open palms facing forward or sit with your hands resting on your thighs with open palms facing up. If you are lying down, let your arms rest either side of you with open palms facing up.

––––––––––––––––

To begin, do the opening practice of the Microcosmic Orbit, as described above (*see* p.114), down to the perineum. Then continue as follows.

Down to the Feet

* As you breathe out, send your mind and energy down the inside of your legs to the area above your knees. Hold your attention there. Breathe.

* Breathing out again, send your attention to the area on the inside of your leg just below your knees. Hold your attention there.

* Now send your awareness and energy down to the area just below the inside of your ankles. Hold your attention there.

* Finally, send your concentration to the area on the soles of your feet, in the centre just behind the balls of your toes.

Up to your Neck and Shoulders

* As you breathe in, draw your mind and energy up to the area just below the outside of your ankles. Hold your attention there. Breathe out.

* Then, breathing in, draw your energy up to the area just below the knee, on the outside of your lower leg. Hold your attention there.

* Next, bring your energy and awareness from the outside of the knee up the back of the leg and then across to your perineum. Hold your attention there.

* As you breathe in, draw your attention up the centre line of your back, along the spine, to the point where your neck and shoulders meet. Hold your attention there.

Down the Outside of your Arms

* As you breathe out, send your mind down the back of your arms to the outside crease of your elbows. Hold your attention there.

* Then, send your attention down to the outside of your lower arms, to where the two bones of your forearms meet, a couple of inches (5 cm) above the centre of the fold of the crease of your wrist. Hold your attention there.

Up the Inside of your Arms

• Now, move your mind and energy to the middle and centre of your palms at the Lao Gong point. Hold your attention there.

• Then, bring your attention up to the centre of the inside crease of your wrists. Hold your attention there.

• Next, continue moving your energy up to the middle of the inside crease of your elbows. Hold your attention there.

• Then move your energy up to the 'valley' where the front shoulders meet your rib cage, just below where the collar-bones meet the top of your arm. Hold your attention there.

Over your Shoulders to the Top of your Head

• Continue by directing your energy up to the top of the shoulders, on the middle of the mound of the shoulder muscle. Hold your attention there.

• Now, bring your attention and mind up the sides of the neck, to the area in the hollows at the base of the skull, in the valleys between the two sets of muscles there. Hold your attention there.

• Now bring the energy from both left and right sides together, at the middle of the base of your skull. Hold your attention there.

• Next, bring your mind and energy to the crown of your head. Hold your attention there.

Back to your Navel

* Finally, as in the Microcosmic Orbit, connect the tip of your tongue to the roof of your mouth, then bring the energy down the centre line of the front of your torso back to your navel.

To Continue

* You can repeat this sequence 3, 9 or more times.

To Close Down and Finish

* To seal your energy at your navel, spiral out and back in, starting clockwise/left for men and counter-clockwise/right for women. It is important to do this so that you are not left open and vulnerable to negative external energy.
* Pay attention to how you now feel. Remember and record this, either in your mind, as a word or image, or write it down in a journal.
* Slowly open your eyes and return to the outside world.

You have now completed a version of the Macrocosmic Orbit. This is also called 'the Greater Heavenly Cycle'. There are a number of variations of this practice and a range of styles taught by different teachers.

Summary

The preceding exercises are adaptations and modifications of some well known and treasured Chi Kung classics. Variations of these practices have been developed over the centuries. They can be done individually or can be performed in one continuous sequence. They are simple procedures which use the body's natural postures and movements to increase and refine body energy. They are very powerful and effective if performed correctly, and will enrich the energy of anybody who will simply take the time, focus their attention and learn these practices, and do them.

Chapter Six

Instant Energy – for Work, Home and Play

- Introduction
- Reverse Breathing
- The Six Healing Sounds
- Drawing External Energy into You
- Supercharging your Power Centre
- Bringing in the Changes
- Tree Kung
- Summary

气 功

Chapter Six

Instant Energy – for Work, Home and Play

Introduction

If we do not know how to feel, read or measure our energy, we cannot have any idea what state it is in, or what actions or adjustments to make. If we do not know how to control our energy we can end up like a dripping tap or a bucket with a hole in it – instead of feeling fully charged and full of life, we feel weak and depleted.

Because of the lack of this knowledge and awareness some people are like used-up 9-volt batteries which just manage to get a tiny bulb to flicker on and off, or faintly run a small transistor radio. We call this 'being tired'. Chi Kung Masters are like mega-volt batteries which can start diesel trains or power huge searchlights. They are like this because they practise.

Regular practice will slowly but surely begin to accumulate larger amounts of energy, develop control and teach how to read energy, what to do, and when. Practice will keep the energy – and the practitioner – strong and clear.

However, keeping your energy in good shape in contemporary society has its problems. Life in the West at the end of the twentieth century is tough, not because of the sheer physical hardships which besieged our forefathers and mothers (thanks to Western science and technology we have figured out a large part of that), but because of pressure and incessant demands. If it's not one thing, it's another. We call this 'stress'.

Most people today suffer, to one degree or another, from stress. Stress is even a medical diagnosis, reimbursable by insurance companies. Everybody knows what stress feels like, but what does it mean? The best definition that I have come across is: 'Stress is when a person does not get back to neutral.' That is, stress is when someone can't get back to a state of being where everything is effortlessly doing what it is supposed to be doing and working in the way it is supposed to work.

When somebody is not in 'neutral' they do not have the correct balance, flow, quality and volume of their energy. The remedy for most people is to 'take a break', 'get away from it all', 'R&R – re-st and re-laxation'. What does this 're-' mean? It means getting back – re-turning – to neutral, to the Tao. It is like pushing the 're-set' button.

A person feels 'good' when everything is working right. The better the energy works, the better they feel.

Sounds simple? *Well, it is.*

The only problem is knowing how to do what, and when.

The following series of simple practices can help to get the energy system, and the person, back into neutral. These exercises will help re-balance, re-charge and re-fresh. Try them and see.

Reverse Breathing

Most people don't breathe efficiently. Breathing is one of your two main sources of energy, along with eating. When you breathe you take in oxygen (the energy of Heaven), which combines with food (the energy of Earth), like air and fuel in a carburettor, to form the essential energy that you run on.

Many people take short, shallow breaths using only the top section of their lungs. They do not fill their lung capacity with every breath and therefore operate at significantly less than a maximum level. When you breathe, do so fully, with the whole area of the lungs expanding in every direction. When you breathe out, do so as completely as possible.

In Chi Kung there is a breathing technique which deliberately and consciously uses breathing to increase and accumulate energy. This is called 'reverse breathing'.

Standing, sitting or lying.

- As you breathe in, pay attention to, and become aware of, the expansion which takes place in your lower abdomen.
- Your lungs expand as a result of your diaphragm moving downwards, thereby drawing in air and oxygen.
- Normally as you inhale, your lower abdomen expands outwards, as the diaphragm moves down. Reverse breathing involves reversing this pattern.
- Now, try this. As you breathe in, put your attention into your lower abdomen, 2–3 inches (5–7 cm) below your navel; this is your lower energy field, the Lower Tan Tien. As you breathe in, hold your attention and mind at this point and consciously contract the muscles in your lower abdomen. This functions like a weight-lifter lifting weights. The more pressure and tension you put into a given area, the stronger it becomes. Repeat this as much as you feel the need.
- As you breathe out, let your lower abdomen relax and expand.

It is best to do this practice with your eyes closed, but if that is not possible, because you are driving, working or engaged in a conversation, it can just as well be done with your eyes open – and nobody will know that you're doing it. Do it for as long as you feel comfortable.

This practice builds strength in the Lower Tan Tien. Do it any time you want to replenish and increase your energy resources. See how it makes you feel.

The Six Healing Sounds

Sound is a vibrational frequency which reverberates through the tissues and organs of the body. Different sounds have different frequencies, which affect specific organs and functions. Colours also have their individual vibrational frequencies.

One of the main causes of problems, symptoms and illness is stagnation in the various organs and tissues. This in turn can cause a condition of internal heat, which inhibits the organs and functions from operating correctly.

Chi Kung practices have been developed which use sound to release, discharge and expel this energy stagnation. These practices are known as the Six Healing Sounds. They also involve the relationship of the various sounds to the various internal organs and which sense organs each sound relates to. Many variations have developed over the centuries. Usually they are linked to specific postures and movements, which are extensive and complex.

The following practice is a modified and adapted form of the Six Healing Sounds. One of the best things about it is that it can be done sub-vocally, without making any actual noise, and therefore is ideal for practising in a busy office or in a grocery store queue. (A friend of mine, Morton Walker, a medical doctor and author, after returning from a trip to China to study Chi Kung tried using full-throated sounds in the morning in his suburban American home, just as he had seen everywhere he travelled. His house ended up surrounded by police, with guns drawn.)

Each organ has a related sense organ, associated colour and emotion, as described in the Table of Correspondences. These are listed in the following exercises. Do these practices at least three times each, or more if you wish.

Standing, sitting or lying down.

Lungs and Colon/Nose

Breathe in deeply, and as you slowly breathe out release the sound 'SSSSSSS' silently, while letting *white* energy exit through your nose. The emotion is grief.

Kidneys and Bladder/Ears

Breathe in deeply, and as you breathe out release the sound 'HOOOOOOO' silently, while letting *blue/black* energy exit through your ears. The emotion is fear.

Liver and Gall Bladder/Eyes

Breathe in deeply, and as you breathe out release the sound 'SHHHHHH' silently, while letting *green* energy exit through your eyes. The emotion is anger.

Heart, Pericardium and Small Intestine/Tongue

Breathe in deeply, and as your breathe out release the sound 'HAAAWWWW' silently, while letting *red* energy exit through your tongue. The emotion is anxiety.

Spleen and Stomach/Mouth

Breathe in deeply, and as you breathe out release the sound of 'WHHHOOOOO' silently, while letting *yellow* energy exit through your mouth cavity. The emotion is worry.

Triple Heater/No Specific Sense Organ

Breathe in deeply, and as you breathe out release the sound of 'HHHEEEEE' silently, while letting *red* energy leave through your mouth. The emotion is hastiness.

After doing these practices you may feel lighter, cooler, calmer and refreshed.

Do these Six Healing Sounds any time you feel the need to discharge stagnant energy and emotions. Doing them at night, before going to bed, can greatly add to your relaxation and sleep.

Drawing External Energy into You

The energy in the body is not distributed evenly – it is not at the same intensity and power and volume in each place. One of the major energy areas is in the palms, in the energy point known as Lao Gong (as described in Chapter 2). This point in the centre of the palms is a very powerful and potent area; as already mentioned, it is the major point used in Chi Kung healing to transmit energy from the practitioner to the patient. However, apart from being used to transmit energy, the Lao Gong point can also be used to draw energy into you from the outside. This is like breathing in through your palms.

It is best to find a place outdoors where there is natural growth. If you are in the countryside then you are already surrounded by it. If you are in a city, a garden or park will do just fine. If you are in a building, you can do this near a plant or in the sunlight. Pay attention to, and feel, the different qualities and kinds of energy coming from different sources.

Find a quiet place and time. Calm your mind. Even your breathing.

- Open your palms and face them towards the selected energy source. This could be a mountain, lightning, sunlight, grass, vegetables...

- As you breathe in, draw the energy from that energy source into you through your palms. Feel this energy slowly and gradually entering you.

- When you breathe out, don't let this energy escape. Hold it with your mind. Seal it in.

- As you breathe in again, continue to draw this energy into you until you have filled yourself with as much as you want.

- See if you can feel the differences between various sources of energy; they are as different as tastes and smells. Try to feel the differences between flowers in a garden. All you have to do is open your hands and take the energy in. Be receptive.

A word of caution: there are lots of different forms of negative, stale, nasty, dirty, filthy, polluted energy in the outside world. To guard against taking this into you, use your mind to create and place filters over your palms that keep out negative energy. You can do it! Just do it with your mind.

Supercharging your Power Centre

The Lower Tan Tien – the Sea of Energy – will now be familiar to you. It is one of the major energy points in the body, the home and seat of your *jing* energy, your essence. It keeps you grounded. Keep your Sea of Energy strong and full, and you will maintain your basic strength and power.

There is a simple way in which you can concentrate, accumulate and bring energy into your Lower Tan Tien. People do this naturally, all the time, without having the slightest idea that they are doing it. You can do this practice sitting down while watching TV, working at a desk, standing up having a conversation or at a formal occasion.

————————————

Standing, sitting or lying.

- Place the palm of one hand on your lower abdomen, on the Lower Tan Tien/the Sea of Energy, so that the centre of the palm – the Lao Gong point – is exactly covering it. Then place the centre of the other palm over the back of the centre of the first palm, so that both Lao Gong points are aligned. One very important issue here is that the polarity is different for men and women. For men the left hand should be on the abdomen, with the right hand on top. For women the right hand should be on the abdomen with the left hand on top.

* Close your eyes if possible, but if that is not appropriate just concentrate your attention inside yourself.

* As you slowly breathe in, also draw energy in through your Lao Gong points to your Lower Tan Tien, using your mind and attention. Feel your Tan Tien get warmer. Let your energy accumulate there and grow strong.

* Continue drawing energy in until you feel recharged or fuller. Hold your energy there with your mind.

* You can control just how much you charge up by mentally adjusting the intensity, strength and volume of your concentration. Get a sense of the percentage of increase and give it a specific number. Try this and see for yourself.

You can use this exercise at any time. Doing it for one minute is much better than not doing it at all. Doing it for five minutes is far better than one minute. The more you practise, the longer you will be able to do it. The longer you do it, the stronger and better it will get. Doing this practice can help make you feel at ease, centred and strong.

Bringing in the Changes

This is a variation of the above exercise. It involves the use of various patterns of connecting your fingers, according to the principles of the Pa Kua (*see* p.59).

You can now create eight variations of touching, and thereby connecting, the tips of the middle three fingers on each hand, with its opposite on the other hand. These are combinations of Yin and Yang. Each configuration consists of a pattern of connected (Yang/unbroken) or unconnected (Yin/broken) lines. The configurations of these three fingers form what is known as a trigram (*see also* p.144). Trigrams are foundational to Oriental philosophy and science; they are a way of understanding the nature of change, of how all situations vary between the limits of positive and negative/full and empty/Yang and Yin. There are eight trigrams in all.

This practice acts in two ways:

1 As a filter for drawing into yourself the eight variations of change, which are the primary energies of the Pa Kua.
2 As a way of instilling these important patterns of change in your mind.

This practice is best done sitting on the edge of a chair, but can also be performed in a standing posture.

• Join the tips of the thumbs and the tips of the little fingers together to form a circle. Do not connect your other three fingers.

- Place the joined tips of the thumbs at the level of the navel, so that the connected tips of the little fingers are 4–8 inches (10–20 cm) (depending on the size of your hands) below your navel on the centre line of your lower abdomen. The mid-point on your abdomen, between your thumbs and little fingers, is your Lower Tan Tien point.
- By touching the three fingertips in their range of combinations you can create the following eight trigrams:

1 Heaven

2 Thunder

3 Water

4 Mountain

5 Earth

6 Wind

7 Fire

8 Lake

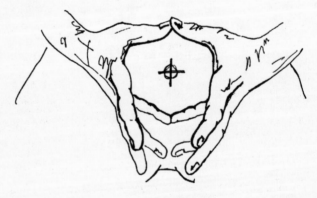

The Lower Tan Tien

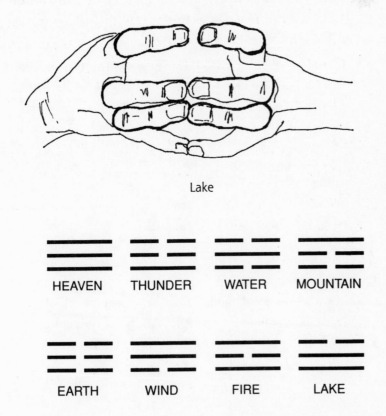

Lake

HEAVEN   THUNDER   WATER   MOUNTAIN

EARTH   WIND   FIRE   LAKE

Connection patterns of top, middle and bottom fingers to form
the eight trigrams

- These configurations act as filters of energy. Each one creates a pattern which 'opens the gateway' and allows one of the eight trigram energies into you.
- Make each trigram one at a time, in sequence. As you make each pattern, hold the essence of the image of the trigram in

your mind – Heaven, Thunder, Water, Mountain, Earth, Wind, Fire, Lake. Draw the energy of that particular trigram into your Lower Tan Tien.

* To end, cover your Lower Tan Tien with your palms, left first for men, right first for women, and breathe in and out there.

You can do this while sitting at your desk, waiting in a reception room, standing at ease at a formal occasion or lying in bed before going to sleep. When done discreetly nobody will notice or pay any attention to what you are doing – they will think you are just fiddling about with your fingers!

Doing this practice not only affects your energy, it also exercises your mind. It brings into your consciousness, and thereby reinforces, the range of patterns of the major variations and possibilities of change. For further study of this profound understanding of the dynamics of change, I refer you to the great classic the *I Ching*.

Tree Kung

And finally, one exercise for doing in private or, for the brave, in public. For this you need one tree. It is best to select a tree which is full, strong and healthy.

Trees have an energy system, just like we do. The major difference is that theirs is less complicated than ours, which is probably to the tree's advantage. Trees stand between Heaven and Earth, a straight connection – roots buried deep into the earth, branches and leaves up in the heavens. It is as if the tree were one big single meridian channel. It is possible to draw the energy from a tree into yourself, like filling up the petrol tank in your car.

_____

To do this practice, stand in front of the tree, close your eyes, clear your mind, calm your breathing and open your energy self.

- With your mind, open the points on the top of your head and the bottoms of both feet. As you breathe in, draw the energies of Heaven and Earth into you, joining them at the point where your neck and shoulders meet.

- Then place the centre of both palms on the trunk of the tree. Open your mind and connect and harmonize your energy with the tree's energy.

- As you breathe in, draw the energy from the tree in through your palms. When you breathe out, seal off your palms with your mind so that you do not leak energy or so that the tree does not draw your energy from you. When you breathe in again, draw in the energy. Repeat this 3 to 15 times.

- With your mind, open the point on your brow between your eyes, Yin Tang, and connect your consciousness directly with the consciousness of the tree (trees, like all living things, have a consciousness). Draw that energy into you. Pay attention to what you feel. If you wish, place your brow point against the tree. Maintain this practice for 2–5 minutes or longer.

• To end, take your hands away from the tree, place your palms over your navel and breathe in there. If you like, you can dance around the tree and thank it for sharing its energy with you.

This practice is a quick, surefire way of recharging yourself. Forget what neighbours or onlookers say – if they ask you what you are doing, tell them about this book and advise them to get a copy. If you are shy about this practice, do it at night, when it's dark!

Summary

The foregoing practices are ones that anybody can do. They will help put your attention inside you, to centre you and make you aware of your energy. There are many other possibilities and variations of such practices. Bear in mind that the main problem that most people have with their energy is that they do not even know that they have an energy system, never mind how it works.

These practices are easy to do and can be done at any time. Use them at work, home and play – for instant energy.

Chapter Seven

Checking the Chi with Just the Mind

气功

Chapter Seven

Checking the Chi with Just your Mind

Introduction

Chi Kung involves different levels of practice, which are developmental and progressive – like any other skill, the more you do it, the better you get.

It starts with physical POSTURES and MOVEMENTS,

which moves on to MEDITATION,

then becomes a process of ENERGY CIRCULATION,

which develops to using just the MIND.

Higher levels require using the SPIRIT.

The ultimate achievement is to ENTER THE VOID,

and thus RETURN TO THE TAO.

This chapter presents a series of practices which can be done using the mind alone. This requires a passive, receptive, observing awareness, without thinking, in order to become aware of what you are feeling and sensing.

A Chi Kung practitioner uses the mind, consciousness and will-power to become aware of the energy – to concentrate attention, to listen and to get the feedback. However, it is not altogether clear how this actually works – there are ways in which this process happens that do not seem to relate to the normal ability of the brain to get information and feedback from the nerve endings.

The usual way that we 'feel' and 'sense', and therefore know what is going on inside us, is by our brain receiving messages through the nervous system. This takes place through what is known in Western anatomy and physiology as the 'proprioceptive system'. But, there seems to be some other way in which we 'read' our energy which is not within the realm of known Western biological science.

From my own personal experience and teaching it seems that rather than being the mind/brain which is reading the body through feedback from the nerves, it is the consciousness (known as Yi to the Chinese) which scans the energy system and can thereby feel, sense and experience it. It could be that we have common and familiar ways of operating through our consciousness which we have not recognized or identified, and that these can be used to experience, read and control the energy system.

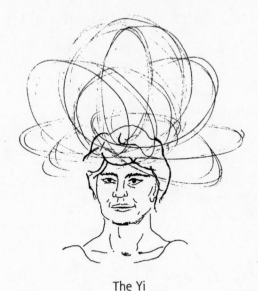

The Yi

The complete energy system consists of three major components:

1 The meridian system – the channels of *chi*/energy which connect the organs and functions.

2 The cauldrons – the energy centres in the vertical core of the body (also known as chakras).

3 The aura – the biomagnetic field which surrounds the body like a cocoon.

In total these can be called the 'energy-body'.

The following practices are designed to help read, check and develop the energy-body, just using the mind and awareness.

Focusing into your Energy Centres

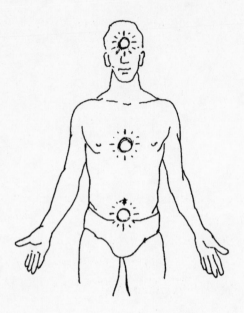

As outlined earlier, the Three Tan Tien are the three major centres of energy. They are places where your energy is accumulated and stored, to feed and nourish your *jing, chi* and *shen* – your essence, energy and spirit. The Three Tan Tien are vital energy centres and need to be full, strong and clear in order for you to feel good. If any of these are depleted, weak or empty you will not feel the necessary level or volume of inner strength and power. You can activate and build these centres through physical postures and movement exercises, but you can also do this with just your mind.

In a standing, sitting or lying position close your eyes, clear your mind and adjust your breathing. Pay attention to how you now feel. Remember it.

The Lower Tan Tien

As you breathe in and out, put your mind and awareness into your Lower Tan Tien, 2–3 inches (5–7 cm) below your navel, on the centre line of your abdomen. Hold it there. Using your mind, draw external energy into you through this point. Feel this grow warm and full. Imagine this as a bowl which is slowly filling with warm water.

Concentrate and fill your mind with the awareness of your deep level essence, your animal vitality, the ancestral energy that you have inherited from your forebears. Let your mind go through the generations upon generations which have gone before you and from which you have descended. Be aware of the enormous vitality of life which has contributed to you being alive right now. Place all of this awareness into your Lower Tan Tien and just let it all be there. Keep your attention in this area for 1, 5, 15 minutes or longer. When you have your eyes closed, keep time by counting your breaths. Four to six deep breaths equal one minute.

The Middle Tan Tien

As you breathe in and out, put your mind and awareness into your Middle Tan Tien, in the centre of your breast bone. Hold your mind there. Draw external energy into you through this point. Feel this grow warm and full. Let it slowly fill until you feel a warm sensation in this area. Pay attention to how this feels.

Concentrate and fill your mind with the awareness of the energy that you gain from eating and breathing, the energy that you run on, that you replenish daily. Be aware of your emotional level and the quality of your feelings, especially of your heart – be aware of the joy, happiness and love that fill your heart when it is at its best. Be aware of the fullness, depth and range of your emotions and feelings. Let these feelings and sensations grow until they feel full, strong and clear. Hold all of this in your Middle Tan Tien and just let it be there. Keep your attention in this area for 1, 5, 15 minutes or longer.

The Upper Tan Tien

As you breathe in and out, put your mind and awareness into your Upper Tan Tien, on the mid-line between your eyes. Hold your mind there. Pay attention to how this feels. Draw external energy into you at this point and feel it become warm. Let this area slowly fill until it is full of energy.

Concentrate and fill this point with the awareness of your mind, consciousness and spirit. This point is known as 'the Original Cavity of the Spirit'. Be aware of the power of consciousness which has illuminated the human mind and spirit throughout history. Be conscious of all of the dimensions of awareness which have emanated from this point in the course of human consciousness. Let this awareness permeate and illuminate your own mind/spirit. Place all of this awareness into your Upper Tan Tien and just let it be there. Keep your attention at this point for 1, 5, 15 minutes or longer.

To Conclude

Finally, divide your attention and mind into three equal parts and put a third of your attention into each of the Three Tan Tien.

Activate all three at once, then balance your attention and mind equally between them.

Savour the sensation of warmth and fullness.

Through doing this practice you can feel and experience the three major dimensions of yourself – your essence, your energy and your spirit, your *jing, chi* and *shen*. This will increase your general energy level, and generate a sense of balance, wholeness and integration of all the primary aspects and dimensions of yourself.

Thinking along your Meridians

The superficial, surface-level, meridian pathways of the 12 major organs run in a circuit from torso, to hands, to head, to feet and back to your torso again. There are groupings of three meridian pathways in each of these separate sections:

- From the torso to the fingers, down the inside of the arms, run the meridians of the heart, pericardium and lungs. These are Yin meridians.

- From the fingers up the outside of the arms and shoulders to the head run the meridians of the small intestine, triple heater and colon. These are Yang meridians.

- From the head down the back and sides of the body to the toes run the meridians of the bladder, gall bladder and stomach. These are Yang meridians.

- From the toes up the inside of the legs and the front of the torso run the meridians of the kidneys, liver and spleen. These are Yin meridians.

These meridians are mirror images, equally balanced on both sides of the body.

It is preferable to do this practice while standing, with open palms facing forward. It can also be performed sitting, with your arms hanging down by your sides, palms facing forward. Use your breath as a guide for your mind and awareness.

Arm Yin Meridians – Heart/Pericardium/Lungs

As you breathe in, concentrate your mind and energy under both armpits, letting the space under your armpits expand slightly. As you breathe out, slowly send your energy down the inside of both arms to your fingertips, feeling your energy as it moves down your arms. Repeat this three times or more if you wish. Be aware of any sensation of warmth or tingling in your hands and fingertips.

Arm Yang Meridians – Small Intestine/Triple Heater/Colon

As you breathe in, slowly bring your energy up the outside of both arms up to the sides of your face and head, feeling your energy as it goes. Be aware of any sensation of warmth or tingling. Repeat this three times or more, drawing the energy up your arms to your face and head each time you breathe in. Be aware of how this feels.

Leg Yang Meridians – Bladder/Gall Bladder/Stomach

As you breathe out, slowly send your energy down the back and sides of your head, neck, back and legs to the tips of your toes, feeling this energy as it goes. Repeat this three times or more if you wish. Be aware of any sensation that you feel. Be aware of any feeling of warmth or tingling in your feet and toes.

Leg Yin Meridians – Kidneys/Liver/Spleen

As you breathe in, slowly bring your energy up the inside of your legs and up the front of your body, to your chest and armpits, feeling this energy as it moves. Repeat this three times or more. Be aware of any sensation of warmth or tingling that you feel on the front and sides of your chest or in your armpits.

---

* Be aware of how you now feel in total. Remember this feeling and sensation. Find a word, phrase, image or symbol to describe it.

* Repeat this whole sequence 3, 6, 9 or more times.

* Run through the whole sequence in one continuous flow within the time of two exhalations and inhalations – exhale down the inside arms, inhale up the outside arms, exhale

down to the toes, inhale back up to the torso. This takes less than one minute. Repeat this sequence three or more times.

• To end, bring your energy from both armpits to the front of the base of your throat as you breathe in, and then as you breathe out send your energy down the centre line to your navel. Hold it there. Place your palms over your navel – left first for men, right first for women – and seal your energy in.

• Pay attention to how you now feel. Remember this feeling.

This practice helps run your energy along the major organ meridians, and to keep it even, smooth and flowing.

Opening the Major Chi Kung Points

There are 12 major Chi Kung points, out of the 670 plus total acupoints on the body. These are 1) the crown, 2) the perineum, 3) the navel, 4) the point opposite the navel on the back, 5) the centre of the chest, 6) the point opposite it on the back, 7 and 8) the centre of the palms, 9) and 10) the centre of the soles of the feet, and 11) the brow. 12) The tip of the tongue connecting with the roof of the mouth behind the teeth is also considered a major point.

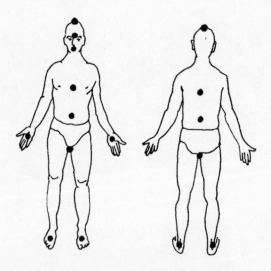

Opening the major Chi Kung points

You are going to open and activate these 12 major Chi Kung points sequentially, so that they will all end up turned on at the same time.

To do this practice requires using the percentage scale (as described in the Appendix, *see* p.211). You hold your awareness/mind simultaneously in different places, with varying proportions of attention. When you add an additional point to the ones that are already activated, you must adjust your mental percentage scale so that the sum total of your attention is equally divided among all of the points together. For example, if you are focused on two points, the percentage of attention to each point is 50 per cent in each. If you are focused on four points, the percentage is 25 per cent in each, and so on. When the percentages get obscure – for instance 14.2 per cent when you have seven points activated – just trust your mind to do this correctly.

To begin, stand, sit or lie down. Close your eyes, calm your mind and regulate your breathing. Have the palms of your hands open – facing forward if standing, resting on your thighs facing upwards if sitting, or resting by your sides if lying.

- Check out how you feel. Take a mental snapshot and file it away in your memory for comparison later.
- Focus your mind and awareness and hold it at each of the following points for three breaths or longer.
- Connect the tip of your tongue to the roof of your mouth, just behind your teeth.
- Focus on your navel. Breathe in and out.
- Focus on the back point opposite your navel. Breathe in and out.
- Focus on your crown point. Breathe in and out.
- Focus on your perineum point. Breathe in and out.

- Focus on your palm points. Breathe in and out.
- Focus on the points on the soles of your feet. Breathe in and out.
- Focus on your heart point in the centre of your chest. Breathe in and out.
- Focus on the point on your back opposite your heart. Breathe in and out.
- Focus on your brow point. Breathe in and out.
- Now, be aware of all of these points being open, activated and turned on at the same time. See them as lights, all lit up. Feel your energy in them.
- Pay attention to how you feel now. Take a mental snapshot of this feeling. Compare this to the snapshot you took before you began this practice. Note the difference. Remember this.

To end there are two possibilities:

1 Go back through the sequence in reverse order, closing one point down after the other, until you end up back at your tongue, then disconnect your tongue from the roof of your mouth.
2 Slowly turn down the volume and intensity of all of the points at the same time, as if you were turning down the dimmer on a light switch. Finally, just click it off.

When you have turned your energy off, open your eyes again and return your attention to the outside. Check how you now feel.

There are other possibilities of how to open up and turn on these points. You don't even need to turn all of the points on, just the ones you want or need. Once you have done the above sequence, experiment and try other options yourself.

You may use this practice to activate and increase your energy at any time.

Scanning the Whole Energy-Body

The human body is like a simple bar magnet, with a positive pole at one end and a negative pole at the other. The central core of the body is the Thrusting Channel/Chong Mo, which runs from your crown to your perineum. Along this channel are seven major centres of energy known as 'cauldrons' (more familiarly referred to as the 'chakras' of the yoga system). Around and outside the body is a bio-electromagnetic field, similar to the energetic field surrounding a bar magnet. The Chinese refer to this field as Wei Qi, but it is more commonly known in the West as the 'aura'.

Your aura is an extension and reflection of your energy system. It is said to have seven distinct levels of refinement, each one corresponding to one of the seven cauldrons/chakras. The lowest cauldron relates to the first aura level, closest to the body, while the highest cauldron relates to the outermost aura level, the one furthest from the body.

Your aura is like an antenna – it connects you with subtle external energy. For instance, it resonates with the Earth's magnetic field. It is most important for your health and well-being to keep your aura clear, clean and strong. Your aura reflects and affects your meridian energy, and can be beneficial or detrimental to all of your organs, functions and overall health.

The following practice can help you check, clear and balance your whole field and also repair any irregularities or disturbances in your energy system. Checking your aura field can put you back in good order and prevent imbalances before they become physical problems.

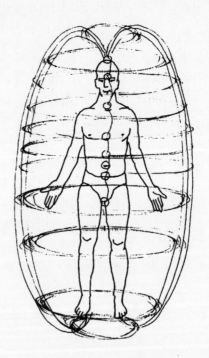

In this practice you use your awareness to 'scan' your body-energy field, like a personal internal radar.

This practice is performed in a standing position, arms by your sides with open palms facing forward.

- Begin by focusing at your navel, then spiral out and in to open and activate your centre, as explained on pp.164–165.

- Using your mind and intention to direct your energy, start at the level of your navel. Beginning at the central core at the Thrusting Channel, spiral horizontally level with the ground, around to your left. Over the course of nine rotations gradually increase the size of the spirals past the surface level of your skin and then out to the edge of your aura field, to end at the outermost edge of the furthest field directly in front of you. When you have reached this point, come directly back to the starting-point at the inner core of your Thrusting Channel.

- Slowly spiral upwards to the left and as you go up let your mind scan through horizontal cross-sections of the complete diameter of your whole field. Pay close attention to how you feel and what you sense. Do this carefully and get feedback. Pay attention to what this feedback means. Use your intuition, your 'sixth sense'. If your energy is slow or stuck, empty or uneven, too heavy or too light, use your mind to gently but firmly put it right, then continue.

- Continue on up to your crown, then hold your energy there for as long as you feel the need to.

• Now reverse the direction of the spiral, turning it to your right, and move it down your body.

• Move on down past the navel, the perineum and the knees to end at the soles of your feet, scanning as you go, and stopping where you notice any irregularity to do whatever is needed. Finally bring the spiralling to a halt on the soles of your feet.

• Again, reverse the direction so that you are now spiralling to the left once more, and bring it up your legs and torso, back to your navel.

• Finally close down your navel by reversing the spiralling pattern above and below your navel that you began this practice with, but this time spiralling in the opposite direction to the one you began with. Men turn to the left/clockwise, women turn to the right/counter-clockwise.

• Pay attention to how you now feel.

This practice strengthens and clears your aura. It acts as a protective shield, an envelope, an energy 'overcoat' to keep out undesirable energetic, psychic and emotional influences. There are different ways of doing the practice – you can slow down and do the spirals closer together and in more detail, or you can open them up as one big cocoon.

Begin slowly, learn it carefully and you will be able to turn your aura on whenever you wish or need to. It will make you feel wonderful!

Drawing Heaven and Earth into You

One of the primary principles of the Chinese world-view is that of 'Heaven–Earth–Human'. This statement may seem self-evident, but its simplicity conveys a profound truth.

Heaven means everything above us – sunlight, sky, clouds, moon, sun, the heavenly bodies, galaxies. Heaven is the primary Yang.

Earth means everything on this planet and the Earth itself – plants, trees, other creatures, mountains, oceans, continents, right on down to the molten core. Earth is the basic Yin.

As human beings we stand between Heaven and Earth, between Yang and Yin.

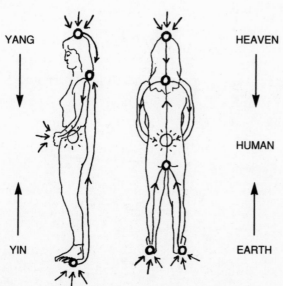

Drawing heaven and earth into you

Stand, sit or lie in a relaxed and receptive posture. Close your eyes or just keep them partly closed. Focus inside yourself.

- Place your hands over your Lower Tan Tien – left first for men, right first for women.
- Put your mind into your navel, and open it.
- Put your mind into your crown, and open it.
- Put your mind into the two points on the soles of your feet, the Bubbling Spring, and open them.
- Slowly breathe in, and as you do so draw the energy of Heaven – sunlight, climate, the moon, planets, stars, cosmos – to the crown point on the very top of your head. Collect your energy at this point. When you breathe out, hold this energy, do not let it go.
- As you breathe in, draw the energy of Earth – the ground, plants, water, metal, minerals – to the point on the soles of your feet. Collect the energy there. When you breathe out, hold this energy, do not let go of it.
- As you breathe in, draw the energy of Heaven from your crown down the centre line of the back of your head to the point where your neck and shoulders meet. This point is known as Da Zhui/Great Hammer.
- As you breathe in, draw the energy of Earth from the soles of your feet up the back of your legs to the back of your pelvis, then up the centre line of your back to this same point where your neck and shoulders meet.

- Gather and combine the energies of Heaven and Earth at this point. Pay attention to how this feels. Hold your attention and energy there. Slowly and deeply breathe in, and each time you breathe in draw energy to this point. When you breathe out, just keep your mind and energy concentrated there; don't let the energy disperse. Let it build and accumulate until the point feels full.

- Now, as you breathe out, send the energy down both arms to the Lao Gong points in the centre of your palms and then through your palms to enter your Lower Tan Tien. Gather your energy there. Take it in. Let it soak into you.

- You can also do this practice with your hands 6–12 inches (15–30 cm) away from your body, with your Lao Gong point in the centre of your palms directed at this same point.

- Pay attention to how this feels. Find a word, an image, a picture or a symbol to describe this sensation. Remember it.

- When you have finished, slowly open your eyes and return to the outside world.

Once you have learned this practice and have become proficient in it, you can do it when you are touching somebody (a loved one, a child, giving a massage, practising acupuncture, healing touch, therapeutic touch, and so on), or when engaged in some other activities (working, gardening, cooking, cleaning, and so on).

Doing this practice plugs you into the universal 'mains'. You draw Heaven and Earth directly into yourself.

Summary

The practices presented here can help you gain control of your energy by using the mind alone. They are a way to check yourself. By applying purposeful intent, practising slowly and paying careful attention to the feedback, you can learn to 'read' your own energy.

You will also get the sense of what needs to be done to correct any irregularities or disturbances in your energy system. Doing these practices is like getting preventive acupuncture – taking care of things *before* they become problems.

These practices can be done at any time, anywhere, as and when needed. Some can even be done without other people knowing. They can be done at work. They can be done alone at home in the privacy of your own bedroom. They can be done during social situations. They can even be done waiting to pay at the supermarket.

With practice you can get to a stage where the practices are happening automatically, for they are built into the normal awareness and consciousness so deeply that they naturally keep your energy functioning at its best.

You can also begin to learn what effect people, places and situations are having on you by being able to 'read' the effect on your own energy. And when your energy is out of order, you can put it right again.

Our energy is the power which connects everything and makes sense of it all. Our energy system is the intermediary between our minds, bodies, emotions, soul and spirit. When we have our energy working correctly – when it is balanced and free flowing, with the right quality and good volume – then we are in our best state and give ourselves the best options. Chi Kung teaches you how to do this.

When someone practises Chi Kung they will be better in every way. It is one of the best things that anybody can do for themselves. It is a way to realize your total energy potential – and the fullest amount of life! All you have to do is practise...

Chapter Eight

The Future of Chi Kung

- Medicine
- Sport and Athletics
- Recreation
- Art
- Education
- Psychology and Mental Health
- Social Services
- Business
- The Environment and Ecology
- Sex
- Anti-Ageing
- Personal Development
- Summary

气 功

Chapter Eight

The Future of Chi Kung

The future of Chi Kung looks vast. Given that what we are dealing with here is life itself, we have a wide range of possibilities as it enters the West and becomes part of our culture.

There are many possibilities because there are many kinds of Chi Kung. It is comparable to music, dance or painting – there are many aspects, with a wide variety of purposes. Just as there is music for entertainment, for relaxing, for aerobics, for military marches, for fun, for loving, for spiritual worship, etc., so there are different forms of Chi Kung for different applications. The type of Chi Kung a person does depends on the reasons for doing it, the intent and purpose.

The main applications of Chi Kung are for fitness, sport, martial arts, health and healing, sex, longevity, extraordinary abilities, spiritual development and immortality training. Each of these areas of application has its own practices and its own specific sequences of training, although in some sense there is a continual developmental spectrum from fitness to spiritual development.

How this range of possibilities will graft onto our own established culture remains to be seen, but the following gives a sense of what might unfold. As usual, though, things will happen that nobody has ever imagined!

Medicine

Most probably the way Chi Kung will be most widely introduced to the West is through its truly remarkable application in the fields of health and healing. This is because, quite simply, Chi Kung works.

In 1993, when my wife Damaris and I attended the World Conference for Academic Exchange of Medical Chi Kung in Beijing, we heard presentations on an extraordinarily wide range of topics on medical research and treatment currently being conducted in hospitals, clinics and medical centres in the People's Republic and also the rest of Asia. The frontiers of medicine are being extended in China, through Chi Kung.

There are two main categories of Chi Kung as healing. One is self-healing, as already described. The other is external healing, which up until this last decade has been performed exclusively by a practitioner on a patient. Recently, however, as a result of scientific and technical research, instruments have been developed which replicate the radiation from a Chi Kung healer. One such instrument is the Infratonic Qigong Machine, developed in China, which duplicates the infrasonic wavelengths emitted by Chi Kung healers, and which is now extensively used for medical purposes.

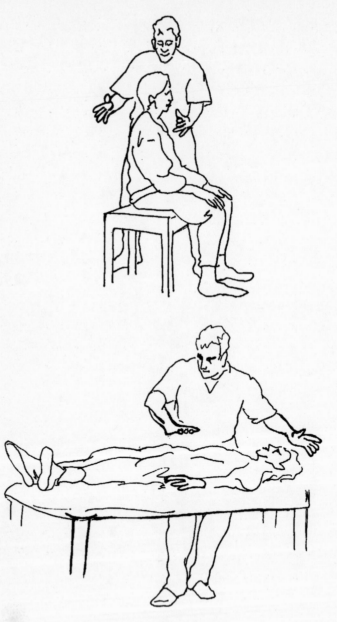

External energy healing

The Future of Chi Kung

The efficacy of Chi Kung in medical treatment is being tested by such research pioneers as Prof. Feng, Li Da, MD. I was in a party of six people who visited her research laboratory in the Navy Hospital in Beijing. She showed data, photographs, slides and electron microscope pictures of the effects of emitted *chi* – everything from increasing the growth rate of plants to the destruction of cancer cells. Apparently this is caused by the emission by a practitioner of infra-red wavelengths, which blast holes in the walls of tumours, killing them. The professor explained that it is possible for a practitioner to 'charge' acupuncture needles, small cloths and other inanimate material with healing energy which can then be used at a later date or sent to some other location. Such 'energy transmission' or 'Chikungization' can have specific purposes – for children, old people, certain diseases, and so on. Prof. Feng gave each of us a single tea-bag which had been charged by a Chi Kung practitioner – Chi tea. I still have mine; I'm saving it for a nice day.

Wondering whether Chi Kung will become part of the health-care system in the West feels a little reminiscent of a few years ago, when I was wondering whether acupuncture would become accepted and established. Yet it is inevitable – for the simple, straightforward reason that it works. It's only a matter of when and how, and who gets to set the rules. Like water following the Tao of its essence, Chi Kung will, without question, find its correct and appropriate level.

Sport and Athletics

Fitness in China is not a fad or a craze, it is a part of everyday life. People are aware of their *chi* and its relationship to fitness and health; it is an integral part of their everyday life, as self-evident as the clothes they are wearing. I suspect that there are some contemporary-style 'health clubs' in some of the hotels for foreigners in China, but for the ordinary people exercise is a public, and a social, affair. Nobody is self-conscious about performing their special routines in public, because everybody else is doing it too, sometimes in very large groups, and they have been doing so for the whole of history. Unsurprisingly, in China people are fitter, and stay younger, longer.

Another aspect of this is that martial arts (Wu Shu), formerly a source of personal and political power and often used in lethal combat, have been transformed in China into what is now called 'physical culture'. This has become a performance art. A practitioner will perform a 'set' in front of a large audience and finish with a bow to applause. It is not unheard of for somebody totally unknown to step into the centre of a circle of people, perform a sequence never before seen, or even imagined, then disappear, never to be seen again.

In the West, sports are a major part of many people's lives; they are often the only time that people engage in vigorous and strenuous physical activity. Every newspaper has a sports section and sports reports appear in every TV news broadcast. For some people sport is the very purpose of their lives. It is also a release for the inherent competitiveness between human beings, the Yang – and it sure beats fighting and wars. The rules and rituals of the 'game of sport' are many-faceted and highly developed, involving play, morality, competition, co-operation, power, strength, tribal warfare, endurance, fun, skill and excellence. But they don't often involve the awareness and application of energy.

Chi Kung will become widespread in the fields of sports and athletics, however, simply because the energy system underlies everything, including strength, power, flexibility, stamina, endurance and speed. In the arena of professional sport, such attributes are the very currency of exchange – and the 'best' win the prizes. So, it would hardly be a surprise if Chi Kung, which improves every aspect of physical performance, were suddenly to appear in training programmes everywhere. After all, it would only take one gold medal/World Cup winner, or one star athlete or head coach, to attribute their success to this strange Oriental movement and meditation stuff for everyone to start doing it, with their kids. Significantly, Chinese athletes have recently begun breaking world records in track events.

There are, of course, two distinct aspects to sports – doing them and watching somebody else do them. Obviously if a person actually plays they get direct benefits to their own body, but how is it that so many people watch so few other people actually playing? Carefully watching the spectators will reveal a strange phenomenon – as well as periodically jumping up and down and generally going nuts when a goal or point is scored, the onlookers often mirror the movements of the players. It is as if they are getting a vicarious work-out through their energy system. I remember watching my father doing all kinds of fancy footwork in football – running at full speed down the wing, dribbling, scoring unbelievable goals – all the while sitting quietly in his armchair watching *Match of the Day* on TV. Perhaps this is why we pay sportspeople so much money – they get to do all the work on our behalf and we get the energy workout!

In the near future, health clubs, aerobics classes, evening institutes and village halls are going to see whole new departments, new programmes and a totally new kind of teacher.

Recreation

Recreation can bring us back into a more balanced, free-flowing energy state and replenish the volume of our energy. As a result we feel better.

I stood outside the gates of Purple Bamboo Park, along with hundreds of Chinese of all ages, at 6.30 a.m. one Sunday morning. Once the park opened most people went to particular locations – groups formed around teachers leading a classic form of Tai Chi Chuan; others were performing with swords; large groups assembled around teachers with boom boxes playing music tapes, like huge aerobic classes (aerobi-kung!); hidden away, in half-privacy behind bushes and in quieter corners, individuals went through their own movements and sequences by themselves, eyes closed, humming or singing, intensely focused inside themselves.

From the other side of the lake, I heard the familiar pounding of loud dance music. On a pavilion extending out over the water dozens of people were dressed in their best, waltzing, doing the foxtrot, the tango... They were also making up their own movements, creatively combining Tai Chi and traditional Chi Kung with dance. When the music stopped everybody would separate, sit down, then a man would elegantly ask a woman for the next dance. It was Saturday night at the Palais on Sunday morning in the park. I was told by a friend living in Beijing that by far the most popular form of Chi Kung practised in the public parks in the major cities in China was not the old traditional forms, but *ballroom dancing!* There are even fierce inter-Asia ballroom formation dance competitions. And why not? You can dress up, it's creative, it's social, it's fun ... and you might just find romance. People are dancing all over Asia.

Next time you dance – whether folk dance, elegant ballroom, performance art or wild boogie – be aware of the energy and the energy fields involved. Dance your energy. Check yourself out. See how you feel. Pay attention to the amount and kind of contact with your partners or group; dance with a soft elastic energy bubble between you. See how it feels with different people and different tempos and rhythms. Do it by yourself in your living-room to your favourite sounds.

Dancing may well be one of the very best things that anybody can possibly do for themselves. It is 'Natural Chi Kung'.

Art

The arts in the Orient are very different from those of the West. They are not examples of individual expression but of emulating style. Painting, theatre, architecture and music all follow prescribed styles and form, and the practitioners' purpose is to see how close to the original form they can stay.

Oriental friends of mine were shocked when they first came to the West and saw films and TV programmes where the actors and actresses were expressing extreme emotions, where, indeed, the whole purpose seemed to be to see just how much emotion a person could have, express and evoke in the audience. This is a completely foreign concept to Orientals, who strive to reach and retain the mid-point of stillness with their emotions and feelings, to get into the centre of them.

This is especially so in the art of calligraphy. In this unique art form it is not *what* a person writes that is so important, it is *how* it is written. What is important is the *chi* of the artist and how this is transmitted onto the paper. To a trained Chinese eye this is as obvious and visible as colour or subject matter would be to us. This is hard for us to understand or appreciate, because there is no comparison in our own culture, primarily because we have had no concept of *chi* as the motivating force of life.

Outside the White Cloud Temple in Beijing, on a wall opposite the front gates, are three enormous calligraphic symbols of great antiquity, which are revered for being written by a very famous calligrapher. They are treated like national treasures. All over China – in public buildings, on walls, in museums – are examples of calligraphy. What is involved here is the spirit of the artist. One stroke of the wrist can express the whole essence of a person. It has been said that Picasso, towards the end of his life when he was doing seemingly simple but astoundingly powerful and moving line and brush drawings, attained the highest level of expression of his essence through his art, in the spirit of calligraphy.

How this emphasis on the cultivation of one's *chi* and its expression in the arts will translate into the West remains to be seen. So far, people in the West who have cultivated their energy to any refined degree have usually done so from the point of view of health or martial arts, not the arts. Perhaps in the West the artistic expression of *chi* will come through music or dance. Perhaps it is already the case but we are just not aware of it, and the reason that some artists stand far out above and beyond the crowd is because they can convey their essence and spirit through their voice or music or movement. Mikhail Baryshnikov, for example, can dance solo on a stage, with no music, and turn otherwise dignified and self-possessed mature and sophisticated adults into drooling and ecstatic fans night after night. Apart from his extraordinary gifts as a dancer, he also 'has the *chi*'. He is a 'Chi Master'. It is his spirit, and his energy essence, that is up there on the stage dancing. And that is what people are connecting with.

Perhaps this will now begin to manifest more widely in our own culture, perhaps we will now begin to develop an art of simplicity, but first people have to learn how to develop and cultivate their *chi* essence. '*Chi* in Western Art' would be an exhibition to look forward to.

Education

The principles, logic and science that Chi Kung is based upon are revolutionary in regard to the way that we think and what we believe to be true. Chi Kung fundamentally changes the basis of what we understand the world to be and how we understand it to operate. This has to become part of how we educate our young.

How can we seriously teach anatomy, for example, without including the energy system – the co-ordinating and integrating system – into the picture? How can we, knowingly, give young people a wrong and outmoded picture of the world? There are relationships between the physical body, seasons, hours of the day, colours, sounds, emotions, temperature, weather, mental functioning and all other phenomena, as described in the Table of Correspondences, and we have a clear obligation to teach this. In the East small children recite songs about the Five Elements, Yin and Yang and the Table of Correspondences, in the same way that children here recite nursery rhymes. It gives them a clear picture, and appreciation, of how everything is integrated and related.

Because it is seen to work, Chi Kung may make it impossible not to include this knowledge into the education system – and hopefully as early as possible. This should not be seen as replacing one system of thinking with another, but rather as additional information, to add to the whole.

Whenever I have taken Chi Kung into the classroom and taught teenagers, they have always been enrapt by the information – to the total astonishment of the teachers. At last, out of all the confusion and chaos of adolescence, here is something that makes sense and ties everything together! Schoolteachers who have studied Chi Kung themselves have taken it back into the classroom and naturally integrated it into the way that they teach and relate to their students. Why? Because it makes sense.

Once we know this information we have an absolute obligation to teach it to children. It's not a weird belief system – it's factual science.

Psychology and Mental Health

Psychology is a new science. It has only been applied for approximately 150 years, but has become fundamental to the way that we think and behave as a culture. It has developed many dimensions, from clinical studies to psychoanalysis used for individual therapy to transpersonal psychology which addresses spiritual issues.

One notable aspect about psychology and psychotherapy is that there is no common agreement about fundamentals. It is as if the field is still at the stage of trying to find out what it really is and how it works. There are many competing and contradictory views. Some aspects of psychology are of immense value – the concept of the unconscious mind; the clarification of beliefs, attitudes and values; understanding our mental processes and use of language, etc. – but other aspects are not of such obvious benefit when looked at from the perspective of Chi Kung.

In the East there has never been a separate field known as psychology – there has never been a separation of the mind and the body and the spirit in this way. The interactions between our physical being, our emotions, our mental level and our spirit are so interrelated that they cannot be separated. In the last 25 years this interdependence has come to be recognized in the West and is now popularly known by the term 'mind, body, spirit', which makes the effort to put back together the three major dimensions of ourselves which were never separate in the first place.

Chi Kung incorporates the Taoist understanding of the rela-tionships between the mind, the emotions and the energy, which in many cases reach the same goal and achieve the same ends as Western psychology – but from a completely different perspective, and at times more effectively. For instance, the relationship of the liver to the emotion of anger is self-evident to any Oriental medicine practitioner. What is not so widely known is that the liver can be checked, cleared, treated and brought into full functioning just by closing the eyes and doing it energetically with the mind. Rather than searching for the underlying historical reasons for a person's actions, and the whys and wherefores and whowiths, the basic approach here is that all that is really relevant is to have things operating correctly in the present time. No amount of talking will 'open' the exit point of the liver, Liver 14/the Gate of Hope, which, when closed, can lead to rage, depression or hopelessness. But people can easily do it themselves, just sitting a chair with their eyes closed, once they know how. The internal 'drives' and 'needs' in a person, and their emotional equilibrium, are as much determined by the condition of their energy as by their mind or beliefs. It seems that this dimension of Chi Kung will prove to have an important impact on contemporary psychology.

Mental health is of supreme importance in a world where one person can hold a whole country to ransom or somebody can go over the top at any time and involve totally innocent victims.

On one hand, we have societies which are perpetually on the brink and prone to widespread random violence that costs more annually than the defence budget. On the other hand, we have a method – Chi Kung – which works to great effect in many situations and a system of training which almost anybody can do. Is there some problem in addition here? Let's see – one and one equals...

Social Services

Although there are many very valuable aspects of contemporary Western society, including social programmes that were undreamed of in the past, there is still enormous room for improvement. The list of social ills is long indeed – juvenile offenders, child abuse, drug addiction, battered women, street gangs, burglary, murder – and there are not many viable answers. A significant amount of these problems stem from such obvious sources as poverty, ignorance, broken families, poor education, lack of opportunity, etc., but how effective are the solutions that are offered? There are a limited number of options provided through social agencies, all of which cost scarce money.

The vast majority of these problems involve emotional disturbance and a significant lack of control by the people involved. Such people are often described as 'unhealthy', 'sick', 'out of control' or 'crazy'. Granted, there are uncorrectable cases of pathological, congenital and psychiatric origin, which need all of the attention and care we can provide, but these apart, most disturbed people would benefit by having their emotions accessible and appropriate, and by having control over their energy.

To know how to cleanse and purify the emotions, and how to cultivate the virtues, would have three distinct benefits:

1 People would be able to correct themselves emotionally *internally*, thus avoiding the externalization of problems into actions, and the intensity of anger, sadness, depression, etc.

2 They would have more 'life' in them and would therefore function better.

3 They would have experience of the Chi Kung state and therefore have different criteria to measure things against.

Chi Kung could become a viable remedy for many social ills. How could this be presented to people? A simple question to ask somebody would be: 'Would you prefer to feel better or worse, in control or out of control?'

Chi Kung should be on the programme of every social service agency and every social worker should be trained in it. Of course, the only way such an unorthodox programme could gain recognition or acceptance would be to try it out and get the results! We need pioneers and clinical studies.

Business

The business world exists to make profits. One of its major resources is people. People work at different levels of efficiency and effectiveness, and any business person in their right mind wants each employee to be working at their maximum. So, the question of what constitutes maximum is of great relevance.

The impact and cost of sickness is an enormous factor that has to be seriously considered in business. In the United States major companies are bringing Chi Kung teachers into the workplace to teach their employees how to relax, de-stress themselves and increase their energy levels. Increased productivity and greater employee satisfaction are the results. As this becomes reflected in profits, no doubt the business world will take every opportunity to utilize Chi Kung.

The executives of business and industry will also become aware of the personal benefits to themselves; after all, it is they who often take the most strain and stress of the job and need to be in the best possible shape. What's more, these people are in a position to initiate change and to create products – machines, equipment and instruments. Now what if a company could produce a *chi* machine that everybody wanted, at an affordable price? It would not be long before a person could go down to the electrical equipment department in their local store and get a few different *chi* machines. So business may be the engine that introduces *chi* into the mainstream. The one thing that can be relied upon in a capitalist society is that if something really works then somebody will make it and lots of people will buy it.

The Environment and Ecology

Ecology is the science of the totality of the patterns of relationships between organisms and the environment. A specific concern for us here is human ecology. There are two major considerations: people's effect on the environment and the effect of the environment on people.

As a species on the planet it is a well known and accepted scientific fact that we are close to disturbing the external environment beyond a critical point. Human-created pollution is degenerating the air, the water, the upper atmosphere and the weather patterns. The soil is polluted. The icecaps are melting. Irreplaceable energy resources are being used up in enormous quantities and the world's population is continuing to grow. The primary requirements for sustaining life are in question. This is serious stuff. Mikhail Gorbachev, the former Russian President who now heads an international think-tank on the environment, has stated that at the current rate of technology and use of resources humankind is heading towards the brink of destruction at the speed of a bullet train. My first reaction to hearing this is to shout, as loudly as possible, *'Put the brake on!'* I believe that Chi Kung is the brake.

The focus of attention in energy usage is usually on the amount of external energy that is being used to sustain our present lifestyle – electricity and petroleum being two major issues. Perhaps the real question is how much energy each person uses for themselves and how much use they make of their inherent energy. If a person's energy system is working properly they will make maximum use of their own energy and use a minimum of external energy. They will make the most use of the energy of the food they eat and the air that they breathe. Some Chi Kung practitioners can eat one meal every couple of days, get four hours sleep and operate at a high-energy level output the rest of the time; periodically, say, every couple of days, they have to get full rest and recuperation – eight hours sleep, like everyone else – but they can operate at much higher levels on much less than people usually do. If people learn how to effectively and efficiently use their own energy they will not be driven to use up vast quantities of external energy. They will not be compelled to find external answers for internal imbalances, but will take care of it themselves just by sitting quietly in a chair and practising. The more people that practise Chi Kung the better for the planet – and for everybody else.

The effect of the environment on people is a different issue. As we grew out of the planet, we are part of it, moulded by its patterns and rhythms. We have evolved totally in the context of, and under the metronome of, energy patterns of the Earth – Gaia. Each person's aura serves as an antenna for these larger energy patterns. We are not only affected by the obvious cycles of day, week, month and year, but also by sun spots, by the cycles around the planet known as the Schumann resonance, by rhythms and oscillations that we are only just becoming able to read and measure now that we have satellites and space stations.

Awareness of the Earth's energy and sensitivity to it have always been inherent. Sacred sites, the locations of stone circles, pyramids, temples, churches and palaces, are long-established healing centres where people have instinctively gone to heal and refresh their souls and spirits – and their body-energy. Hot springs, special mountains, gathering sites – every area of land has them. The energy science of the land has come to be known as 'geomancy' and there is ample evidence that energy lines on the planet's surface, called 'ley lines' (similar to the meridian pathways in the body), congregate at these special places.

Feng shui, which translates as 'wind and water', is an Oriental art which uses the same Taoist principles as Chi Kung and acupuncture, but in relation to the Earth. It is used to place buildings in the most appropriate and propitious locations, taking into account the geography of a given site and its features. It is also extensively used in the placement of interior dynamics and decoration of a home or office. This is one of the reasons for the extraordinary simplicity, beauty and calmness of some Oriental interior design. Feng shui is beginning to become extremely popular in the West and in the future it will not be unusual for a person to get a 'reading' before deciding where to live or how to decorate their environment.

The environment is something that affects every person. Chi Kung is a way that each one of us can be responsible for caring for our common home, planet Earth.

Sex

Sex is one of the most compelling and mysterious natural forces. It is part of our innate biology. It spans the human experience from ecstasy to tragedy. Sexual ignorance, misuse and abuse are some of the primary causes of dissatisfaction in people's lives. In the West we have known almost nothing of the energetic foundation of sex, again because we have never understood the energy system. For us, it is all just some strange kind of 'magnetic attraction'.

Sexuality is a special aspect of Chi Kung. In the broadest sense women are Yin and men are Yang. Yin and Yang balance and complement each other. The interplay of Yin and Yang energy is the basis of sex:

- Men need Yin to balance their Yang.
- Women need Yang to balance their Yin.

However, as the significant portion of society that is homosexual attests to, these balances also operate within same-sex relationships.

Sexual energy is a form of *jing chi*, the innate energy a person inherits from their ancestors. Men have Yang *jing*. Women have Yin *jing*. It is considered essential to preserve your *jing*, as its loss comes at a substantial cost to your overall energy resources. Men are trained not to ejaculate except when they want to procreate, although they can still experience orgasm. Women are taught special techniques to preserve the energy of their menstrual flow, sometimes even stopping menstruation altogether because it is a way they can lose their precious *jing*.

The energy interaction between a couple is called 'dual cultivation'. This may involve a range of interactions from just being in each other's energy field to hugging or kissing or coitus. Through consciously combining and exchanging Yin and Yang it is possible to transform the innate animal level of sex (*jing*) to the emotional level (*chi*) and on up to the spirit (*shen*), and for a couple to spend a lifetime of dual cultivation together, and, hopefully, a lifetime of happiness.

Indeed, it is not even necessary to make physical sexual contact to have this essential balancing and equalizing Yin–Yang energy exchange, if a couple knows how to practise and circulate their energy together. This ability can satisfy the primary needs usually only found through actual sex. It can bypass the many negative aspects of sex and help save people the enormous personal and social turmoil and complications that often goes along with it. Chi Kung can be the ultimate form of safe sex.

For a single individual it is also possible to work with the sexual energy and *jing chi* through what is known as 'sole culti-vation'. People without a partner can cultivate and transform their sexual energy equally well, once they know how.

Without the awareness that sex is a form of energy exchange, it can become a meaningless, emotionally unfulfilling and even draining activity that can cause otherwise good relationships, and families, to fall apart and fail. It can drive people incessantly to seek multiple partners, without satisfaction, or cause compulsive addiction, with all of the attendant problems and dangers.

Chi Kung is the foundation of a developed level of sexuality and answers many of the unresolved questions about this most important aspect of ourselves. As more and more people learn the basics of energy control, circulation and exchange, it may very well be that *chi* becomes the aphrodisiac of the future.

Anti-Ageing

Healthy old age is venerated in China. To grow old and be in good health is a sign that a person has truly understood and followed the Tao, otherwise they would be in bad shape or would not have made it that far. Longevity and anti-ageing practices have a long tradition in Chi Kung.

Apart from the obvious common-sense approaches to preserving health and maintaining youth, there are specific Chi Kung practices which slow down ageing. One of these is known as Bone Marrow Washing, which keeps the marrow free of fat deposits and therefore producing clean, fresh and abundant blood to feed the cells and tissues. Another major aspect involves keeping the energy purified. There are numerous reasons why a person can accumulate 'negative energy' in their system, but they have to get rid of it to be healthy. Some exercises for this are described earlier in this book. If a persons learns these exercises, and does them on a regular and consistent basis, they will live longer and be happier.

In one of the parks in China I saw a group of a dozen older Chinese ladies (who looked in their 60s to 70s but could as easily have been in their 80s) walking, two abreast, along the pathway, nonchalantly chatting with each other, gossiping and laughing, as they all performed the exact same series of hand movements, designed, no doubt, to preserve and strengthen energy and extend longevity. They looked in great shape.

Tai Chi, a specific aspect of Chi Kung which uses movement sequences in a flowing energy dance, is said to be best practised in later years; younger people should practise the more dynamic and powerful forms of Kung Fu and Wu Shu. In Tai Chi the older a person gets, the better they get. There are highly respected teachers who are in their 70s, 80s and 90s, and in playful combat they can toss the young bucks around!

So, if a person learns Chi Kung and follows the Tao, they will not only invest in their present, but also in their old age. With the right practices, old age can be mature and wise and happy ... and truly 'golden'.

One of the problems involved in conveying this in a public sense in the West is that not enough time has passed yet. There are no non-Asian practitioners who were originally trained by their grandparents, as is the rule in the East. The current Western generation of Chi Kung practitioners is the very first.

There are as yet no shining examples of living to a ripe old age in great shape walking amongst us. So again, we lack reference points. However, this problem will be remedied in about 25 years.

Personal Development

There are innumerable reports of people developing extraordinary and sensational abilities through Chi Kung, ranging from unusual feats of strength and endurance to what has commonly come to be known in the West as 'psychic' phenomena. There are many reported instances of the ability to 'read people's minds' and examples of people 'healing at a distance' through just talking on the phone or with nothing more than a name or description. There are also stories of people able to disperse cloud formations by directing their energy at them. (Remember, microwaves, which are part of the cocktail of body-energies, allowed us to talk to guys on the moon!)

These abilities are not easily accounted for or within the realm of normal understanding. However, almost anybody willing and able to undergo the necessary practices can attain such abilities. Such internal processes are, of course, very potent. They bestow significant powers on whoever understands them. They are jealously guarded by the practitioners who know them and are generally kept secret, yet at the current accelerating rate of discovery they may become common knowledge in the not too distant future in the West.

I have frequently had the experience of speaking to somebody who has had their first encounter with an advanced Chi
Kung practitioner or doctor. The conversation echoes a familiar refrain as the person describes how this practitioner seems
to be unique in having refined and admirable attributes – being
gentle, kind, bright, aware, modest, competent, skilled, good-
natured, and so on. My automatic and instinctive response is,
'But they are all like that'. It appears to be a consequence of
developing a mastery of Chi Kung practices that the person
also, inevitably, develops their higher-level attributes as a
human being. This may be partly explained by the fact that the
practices required to be learned in order to progress up the
ladder of development in and of themselves develop the moral
and ethical qualities of the individual. When the energy system
is clean and clear and functioning the way it should be, then
the inherent good qualities of a person spontaneously emerge.

These principles may apply on emotional and social levels,
but there are higher levels than this, which involve the *shen*,
the spirit. From the Oriental point of view this does not have
the same connotations as 'spirit' does in the West. It is understood as being related to the energy-body. If a person's *shen* is
strong it is clearly seen in their eyes – if they have deficient
spirit their eyes are dull and lethargic and there is not much life
or light in them, whereas if the *shen* is strong, the eyes sparkle
and are *alive*.

There is a level of Chi Kung known as 'Inner Alchemy',
which is practised for spiritual development. By gathering,
circulating and refining energy in the right way, practitioners

create an internal 'steam' which is used to gently stimulate the pineal gland, the master gland in the centre of the brain. This is said to release secretions which act as a catalyst and lubricant to the mind and awareness, and which thereby kick it into a higher level of functioning. The stronger the level of energy radiating from these centres, the stronger the spirit.

Chi Kung is one of most effective processes ever developed for realizing human potential.

Summary

As Chi Kung enters the West and becomes established as a part of our culture, it is going to manifest in many ways. How this will all turn out remains to be seen, but some things seem certain:

- It will change the way that we think about ourselves, about what we are and how we function as 'human energy events'.
- It will affect our way of thinking, because to understand it requires a different and expanded way of thinking – Taoist thinking.
- It could give us a new reference point and new criteria to measure ourselves against, and thereby set a new standard for our behaviour and actions.
- It could make what is crazy about our society sane again.

- It could keep us healthy and vital and happy and young and operating at our higher potentials.
- It could make us our best.

Hopefully this list of possibilities will fall far short of the reality and unimaginable benefits will emerge for everyone.

The future will soon be now.

气 功

Afterword

From all of the indications Chi Kung is about to hit the West like a tidal wave. It is likely to transform the way we experience ourselves. It will be like finding a new dimension of ourselves. Hopefully, Chi Kung will not become an overused and misused term which comes to mean almost everything and therefore nothing in particular. Over time standards will be established and people will learn to differentiate between various styles, levels, teachers and practitioners. As Chi Kung becomes accepted and established the most important thing is that the awareness of our energy will filter into common consciousness.

My wish is that this book will inspire people to try some of these practices, learn how to become aware of and pay attention to their energy and how to adjust and improve it, and then find a teacher and progress further, until it becomes part of their being.

Afterword

Consider:

If we operate according to criteria which emphasize maintaining our energy at the right balance, flow, quality and volume, how can we not take good care of ourselves and rise above our transient emotions, wants and desires?

If we are focused on cultivating and transforming our energy-body and spirit, how can we become preoccupied and fixated on our own immediate needs, feelings and personal gratification?

If we see ourselves primarily as part of a delicate interrelationship affected by numerous internal and external energies, how can we separate ourselves from other people, society and nature around us?

Chi Kung is the Tao entering the West, Yin joining with Yang to create one whole. Practising Chi Kung is a process of personal evolution and an act of social responsibility. Chi Kung holds the potential to make us healthy, sane and happy – and truly *Alive with Energy*.

气 功

Appendix

A Language of Energy

A language of energy does not currently exist in the West, but to discuss the experience of Chi Kung we need to develop one.

Without an energy language we have no way of describing and understanding our energy, or how to work with, control or develop it. Without an energy language we are limited to vague, amorphous words and strange gestures, instead of having meaningful, interesting and stimulating dialogues. Without an energy language we cannot discuss our experience with others or compare it with another's experiences.

Language, any form of language – movement, sound, image – is inherent in the structure, the hardware, of our brains; the important issue is how it relates to meaning, which in turn relates to our internal sensations and feelings. A language is a means of expressing and communicating internal feelings and sensations.

Chi Kung takes this one step further by looking at how feelings and sensations are based upon our internal energy states. This could be simply described in the following diagram, which operates in both directions:

Verbal language > < *Meaning* > < *Sensations and feelings* > < *Energy state.*

To develop a usable energy language in the West we need to describe the meaning of the sensations and feelings of various energy states in simple, common and familiar Western terms.

The following is a proposal for an energy language of sensations and feelings, based upon classical Chinese principles of our energy anatomy and physiology, and upon principles I have found to be true through personal practice and teaching.

This outline proposal is presented as a first step in devising a Western energy language, and to initiate and stimulate a dialogue with teachers and practitioners on this important issue. Comments, feedback and contributions are welcomed by the author (*see* Further Information, p. 219).

The four components of an energy language are: Yin and Yang, the Five Elements, the Percentage Scale and Volume Control.

Yin Yang

Yin and Yang are the two basic divisions of everything. They are the polarities. And we mainly know something by comparing and contrasting it with something else. Although there are numerous ways that this could be defined, the three major categories discussed here are quality, movement and position.

Sensations of Quality

Yin	Yang
Light	Heavy
Empty	Full
Weak	Strong
Dull	Tingling
Murky	Clear
Dark	Light

Sensations of Movement

Yin	Yang
Still	Moving
Sinking	Floating
Falling	Rising
Stuck	Flowing
Contracting	Expanding

Sensations of Position

Yin	Yang
Bottom	Top
Below	Above
Down	Up
Right	Left
Front	Back

The above are terms of quality, movement and position which describe something in relationship to its opposite – its Yin and Yang aspect.

The Language of the Five Elements

The Five Elements/Five Phases are basic to the Taoist way of looking at the world. They are a way of understanding the essence of something. They are not in comparison to an opposite, but a description of their own basic irreducible nature.

The following is a description of the Five Elements and the related organs, temperature, colour and direction.

	Wood	**Fire**	**Earth**	**Metal**	**Water**
Organs:	Liver	Heart	Spleen	Lungs	Kidneys
	Gall Bladder	Small Intestine	Stomach	Colon	Bladder
		Pericardum			
		Triple Heater			
Temp:	Warm	Hot	Mild	Cool	Cold
Colour:	Green	Red	Yellow	White	Blue-Black
Direction:	Right	Up	Centre	Left	Down

The Five Elements and their Relationships

_____

These two components of Yin Yang and Five Elements consti-tute the foundation of a language for describing sensations.

For example, a sensation can feel light, rising, strong, clear, on the right side, warm and green, or heavy, sinking, full, at the bottom, murky, cold and blue/black, or flowing, yellow, on the left, mild, smooth and tingling.

Any combination is possible. It is important to pay attention to the experience of a sensation and how it could be described in words. When it is put into language, it can be remembered more easily.

The Percentage Scale

In addition to the above two aspects of classical Taoist thought there is another ability our awareness appears to have which is very important in assessing a sensation or feeling. This is the ability to discern and distinguish relative proportion as a percentage. It is like having an internal scale from 0 per cent to 100 per cent.

This is intuitive, but in the experience of the author it is extraor-dinarily accurate. People know what is going on inside themselves, how much there is of a particular sensation, because it is they them-selves who are experiencing it. There is no other way to assess it.

This can most easily be described in units of quarters, with a scale ranging from 0 to 25 per cent, 25 to 50 per cent, 50 to 75 per cent and 75 to 100 per cent.

However, it is also easily possible to assess this in finer distinctions – 15 per cent, 37 per cent, 62 per cent, etc.

A person can 'read' the amount of energy or sensation in any given place with their mind. They can then divide it up and hold it, again using their mind, in different places for different percentages. For example, close your eyes and put 25 per cent of your attention in the hands, 25 per cent in the feet and 50 per cent in the navel. Now divide it equally in thirds!

Volume Control

We all have the natural ability to change the volume and intensity – the power – with which we do something. Just as it is possible to touch as lightly as a feather, so it is possible to touch like a feather and smash like a sledgehammer. Try both now. Touch your palm so lightly that it's difficult to discern if you've actually touched at all, then use maximum force and power.

Because the mind moves the energy, a person is able to instantaneously decide and modulate the intensity with which they do something. This is important because when someone begins to do the practices it is best to do them lightly and quietly at first. Too much volume or intensity and it all may be too much to handle easily or it may create side-effects. If this happens, turn down the volume, 'back off', decrease the intensity. Later, slowly increase it step by step, staying within the limits of comfort and capacity, until the desired or appropriate level is reached.

———

So, combining Yin and Yang, the Five Elements, the Percentage Scale and Volume Control provides a basis for a language of energy.

Try thinking in these terms and discuss your experiences with others. The questions then become 'What kind of energy?' 'Where is it?' 'What is it doing?' 'What is the difference between one kind of energy and another?'

If we can develop a Western energy language we can talk and learn and share together about one of the most important and fundamental parts of ourselves – our energy and our life – to everybody's benefit.

气 功

Further Information

The Chi Kung School
and The Body-Energy Center

The Body-Energy Center was established in 1989. It is concerned with understanding the Anatomy and Physiology of the Energy-Body, and its relationship to the Soul and the Spirit. The Chi Kung School at The Body-Energy Center was created in 1992 to understand, develop and promote Chi Kung. Our purpose is to teach Chi Kung theory and practices so that people can make them their own. We are socially committed to stimulate the ever-increasing interest in this work, as we believe these lifeskills are of primary importance for peoples health, well-being, sanity and happiness in our global community. Health professionals, lay practitioners and the general public have studied and trained with us.

We offer a wide range of programmes, including individual treatments, classes, workshops and training. These range from one-day, weekend, weekly and week-long residential courses, to one-year certification and multi-year apprenticeship programmes.

We have taught Chi Kung in Acupuncture and Oriental Medicine Schools and given presentations at professional conferences and public events. We host guest teachers and conferences.

Visiting workshops, training and consultations for private groups, educational institutions, businesses, corporations, and medical and health organisations are available by arrangement. Please feel free to enquire for details and to discuss possibilities.

In addition to Chi Kung we offer Seasonal Women's Retreats, The Sounds of Personal Ritual class series, The Body-Energy Practitioner Certification Training Programme, Energy-Body Meditations audio-tapes, and more. Our programme changes, evolves and grows continuously.

Our Mailing List

The current brochure and programme are available on request. To be added to our mailing list, send your name, address, phone number and other relevant information.

The International Chi Kung/Qigong Directory

Chi Kung/Qigong is developing at a rapid pace – at about the same speed as the Internet. Any information listed here will, as likely as not, be out of date by the time the book is published. In order to maintain a continuously updated and current source of information a comprehensive international resource directory and database is published which is available on request. To receive a current copy send $20 US, cheque or money order.

Audio Tapes

Audio cassette tapes of the exercises in this book are available, to guide you through the practices step-by-step in the right way. The Energy-Body Meditations by Damaris Jarboux series is also available.

For further information or details please write, phone or fax:

The Chi Kung School at The Body-Energy Center
P.O. Box 19708
Boulder
Colorado 80308
USA

Tel: USA 303 442 3131
Fax: USA 303 442 3141

Bibliography

Chi Kung/Qigong

Edward C. Chang. *Knocking at the Gate of Life and Other Healing Exercises from China*, Rodale Press, 1985

Mantak and Maneewan Chia. *Awakening Healing Light – Tao Energetic Medicine Of The Future*, 1993, *Fusion Of The Five Elements: 1*, 1989, *Healing Love Through The Tao – Cultivating Female Sexual Energy*, 1986, all published by Healing Tao Books

Mantak and Maneewan Chia. *Taoist Secrets Of Love – Cultivating Male Sexual Energy*, Aurora Press, 1984

Lam Kam Chuen. *The Way of Energy*, Simon & Schuster, 1991

Ming-Dao Deng. *Chronicles of Tao Trilogy, The Wandering Taoist*, 1983, *Seven Bamboo Tablets of the Cloudy Satchel*, 1987, *Gateway to a Vast World*, 1989, all published by Harper & Row, New York

Bruce Kumar Frantzis. *Opening the Energy Gates of your Body*, North Atlantic Books, 1993

Roger Jahnke. *The Most Profound Medicine*, 1988, *The Self-Applied Health Enhancement Methods*, 1989, Health Action Publishing

Guo Rui Jiao. *Qigong Essentials For Health Promotion*, China Today Press, 1990

Bibliography

K'uan Yu Lu (Charles Luk). *Taoist Yoga – Alchemy & Immortality*, 1984, *The Secrets Of Chinese Medicine*, 1984, Samuel Weiser

Hua Ching Ni. *The Book of Changes and the Unchanging Truth*, The Shrine of the Eternal Breath of Tao, 1983

Stuart Alve Olson. *The Jade Emperor's Mind Seal Classic*, Dragon Door, 1992, *Cultivating The Ch'i*, Dragon Door, 1993

Daniel P. Reid. *The Tao of Health, Sex and Longevity*, Simon & Schuster, 1989

Richard Wilhelm. *The Secret of the Golden Flower*, Harcourt Brace, 1962

Kiew Kit Wong. *The Art of Chi Kung*, Element Books, 1993

Jwing-Ming Yang. *Chi Kung – Health & Martial Arts*, 1985, *Roots of Chinese Chi Kung*, 1989, Yang's Martial Arts Association Publication Centre

Enquin Zhang. *Chinese Qigong*, Publishing House of Shanghai College of Traditional Chinese Medicine, 1990

Abstract of Presentations, The Second World Conference On Academic Exchange Of Medical Qigong, The World Academic Society of Medical Qigong, 1993

Further Reading

Harriet Beinfield and Efrem Korngold. *Between Heaven and Earth*, Ballantine Books, 1991

Dan Bensky and John O'Connor. *Acupuncture – a Comprehensive Text*, Eastland Press, 1981

Thomas Cleary. *The Inner Teachings of Taoism*, Shambala, 1986, *Understanding Reality*, University of Hawaii Press, 1987, *Immortal Sisters – Secrets of Taoist Women*, Shambala, 1989

Compilation, Essentials of Chinese Acupuncture, Foreign Languages Press, Beijing, 1980

J. C. Cooper. *Chinese Alchemy – The Taoist Quest For Immortality*, Sterling Publishing, 1990

David Eisenberg. *Encounters With Qi – Exploring Chinese Medicine*, W. W. Norton & Co., 1985

Ted Kaptchuk. *The Web that has no Weaver*, Congdon & Weed, 1983

James Legge. *The I Ching – The Book of Changes*, Dover Publications, 1963

George Leonard. *Mastery*, Dutton, 1990

Thomas Merton. *The Way of Chuang Tzu*, New Directions Paperbook, 1969

Stephen Mitchell. *Tao Te Ching*, HarperCollins, 1988

Further Reading

Joseph Needham. *Science and Civilisation in China*, Cambridge University Press, 1954

Martin Palmer. *The Elements of Taoism*, Element Books, 1991

David Scott and Tony Doubleday. *The Elements of Zen*, Element Books, 1992

David V. Tansley. *Subtle Body – Essence and Shadow*, Thames and Hudson, 1977

Ilza Vieth. *The Yellow Emperor's Classic of Internal Medicine*, University Of California Press, 1966

Katya Walter. *The Tao Of Chaos*, Kairos Centre, 1994

Burton Watson. *Chuang Tzu – Basic Writings*, Columbia University Press, 1964

Richard Wilhelm. *The I Ching or Book Of Changes*, Princeton University Press, 1950

Eva Wong. *Seven Taoist Masters*, Shambala, 1990, *Culti-vating Stillness*, Shambala, 1992.

J. R. Worsley. *Traditional Chinese Acupuncture – Vol. 1. Meridians and Points*, Element Books, 1982, *Traditional Acupuncture – Vol. II. Traditional Diagnosis*, The College of Traditional Chinese Acupuncture, UK, 1990

气 功

Index of Exercises

気 功

Index

Index

Index

Index